Manners

not

Mayhem

A common-sense approach to raising, training
and living with your puppy

Lez Graham M.A.

Published by Braidwood Books
an imprint of Trained for Life.

First published 2018
ISBN 978-0-9570051-7-4

A catalogue record for this book is available from the British Library.

Illustrations by www.tom-kitchen.co.uk
Cover design and typeset in 11pt Marathon-Light by www.deprivedanxiety.com

Contents

Foreword

I am fortunate indeed to have spent over a decade working with Lez Graham in various training and behaviour disciplines; from Gundog Assessments and tests whilst she was completing her Masters Degree, to dog safety education programmes, delivering key note talks to organisations, such as the National Dog Warden Association, the Kennel Club Educational Zone at Crufts, and tutoring, lecturing and delivering educational programmes on many and varied subjects relating to dogs.

We have spent many days, evenings and dog walks together musing on various canine topics. As a dog professional, there are a handful of people whose thoughts and opinions I truly value, and Lez is at the top of that list.

One thing I believe is critical for the reader to know, is that Lez walks her talk. Her dogs, of which I have known five or more, are exceptional; both in behaviour and obedience training. She has truly happy, healthy dogs and has achieved a level of training that most can only be in awe of.

That is reason enough, to read this book, re read this book and follow the advice as closely as you can.

Whilst Lez is known for her revolutionary work within the Gundog community – changing perceptions of the working dog's ability to be a pet in the home and bringing kinder, reward-based methods to a previously notoriously harsh industry, she spends most of her time working with dogs from all other breed groups and types.

From the Dachshund to the Bernese Mountain Dog, she has worked with them all and with many severe behavioural and training issues. A little-known fact is that she has a real penchant for the long-coat Chihuahua and the black German Shepherd Dog, as well as the Gundogs with which she presently shares her home.

Once again, as an author, she has created a masterpiece in Manners not Mayhem - a common-sense approach to raising, training and living with your puppy. Lez has a gift for the written word and her unique writing style immediately endears the reader. It is more akin to chatting to a friend than reading a book. It is an easy, enjoyable read which makes putting the book down very difficult.

From understanding the relevant evolution of dogs and breeds, through raising puppies with children and other dogs, Lez's immense knowledge of the subjects herein shines through. However, she has an ability to just tell the reader what they need to know, not labouring unnecessary information, nor withholding critical advice that has taken her a professional lifetime of study and practice to appreciate.

Whilst there are many authors that know a little about a lot – Lez knows a lot about a lot – her thirst for knowledge knows no bounds and her areas of expertise are vast; most importantly, her practical experience is the base from which she teaches, and which is contained in this book.

A favourite saying that Lez and I adore is *"in theory, there is no difference between theory and practice, in practice there is."*

Lez has theoretical and scientific knowledge in spades and has the practical experience that allows her to separate the wheat from the chaff and deliver truly helpful, appropriate, inspiring and practicable information.

I hope as a reader; whether a new puppy owner or even a seasoned dog owner or canine professional on a journey of discovery, that you will truly value the life's work of study and professional canine behaviour and training practice that the author shares with you.

Finally, I thank Lez for her commitment to our pet dogs of all breeds and types, for sharing her knowledge and passion unreservedly with all who are open to listening.

For those that have found this book at the right time, you are lucky indeed... rest assured that you are on the right road.

Ross McCarthy MA FCFBA MBIPDT MGoDT (MT) AMBPSCA
The London Dog Behaviour Company
A Fellow of The Canine & Feline Behaviour Association.
A member of the British Institute of Professional Dog Trainers, The Guild of Dog Trainers. An associate of the British Police & Services Canine Association.

Acknowledgements

This has got to have been one of the hardest books that I've written, and because of that, it has also been one of the most satisfying and enjoyable...

It might have been because I'd been asked to write it from countless dog trainers and behaviourists, or it might have been because I had to design it in a way that was different from The Pet Gundog series, but it has been a bit of a challenge, that's for sure.

However, once I got past moving home, a broken thumb and writers block, it flowed... and as it flowed it brought with it new concepts which will hopefully make it easier for you and your family to train your puppy.

And for me that's what it's all about, educating the new (and returning) puppy owner and empowering them, *empowering you*, to feel confident training your latest addition to be a wonderful member of your family, to guide you through the stages your puppy will go through in his development and help you through some of the challenges you'll face as he gets there.

Writing a book is always an exciting challenge filled with early mornings and broken sleep, and I've got lots of people to thank for their patience and contributions; for answering those seriously early, 'silly o'clock' texts, as my buzzing brain needed to bounce a concept off someone, and for being understanding while being abandoned at various meals and outings, as the authoring inner 'hermit' took over.

And so, I end my acknowledgements in a way that is only right and proper - giving thanks, appreciation and acknowledgment to everyone who has helped write this book, directly or indirectly.

To all of the puppy owners that I've drank coffee with over the years, to the owners of adolescents who I've laughed and cried with, and to the dog owners that I've met out shopping and have regaled me with their latest dog story. I thank you.

To Ross McCarthy and Jill Stagg, my reality-checking-stabilising 'go-to' friends, and to Ross for writing the foreword. To Dee Steadman, Iris Thompson-Burton, Lee Kayne, Gemma Townsend, Mirjam Coert and Richard Reeve for their snippets of information, to Carl Sutton for the fabulous cover, Tom Kitchen for the wonderful illustrations, Brian Costello and his magic arrow, and to Callum Graham for the endless early morning discussions about the brain.

But no one needs to be thanked as much as Kenny Graham, who has had to put up with broken sleep as I've padded about making notes, listened to me saying the same thing over again as I've tried to find the right words... and for helping me stay grounded...

As much as I might wrestle with a manuscript, he wrestles with the proof reading and editing of it; thank you for keeping me sane with the endless cups of tea and your incredible sense of humour...

Introduction

Getting a puppy is an exciting thing... a grinningly exciting, running around with your t-shirt over your face exciting thing... it's also absolutely terrifying.

Bringing home a new bundle of fluff brings with it responsibility and overwhelm and expense; it's a lifechanging event... but it is fabulous.

If this is your first puppy, *fantastic*, welcome to the wonderful world of the dog... if you've had puppies in the past, welcome back to early mornings, late nights and that wonderful intoxicating puppy smell.

It really doesn't matter how many puppies we've raised, we forget what it's like to have a puppy in the house; we forget that we have to go back to feeding four meals a day, to getting up at four a.m. to toilet the puppy and we forget what terrible timewasters puppies are, as we simply cannot stop watching them.

But let's make no bones about it, puppies, especially in the early months, are hard work. So, I've removed the romantic rose-coloured glasses that we all wear when we get a puppy and I've written about what it's really like to bring home and raise a puppy, to get through those lovely, exciting, stressful months of puppyhood and into that jaw-clenching, joyous phase that is adolescence.

Before we go any further however, a quick note if I may, to say that as with all of my books, I write in the 'gender' that I'm familiar with, so apologies in advance to owners of lovely lasses; my dogs are boys and so, as far as my writing is concerned, all dogs are of the male persuasion.

Oh, and whenever I write 'sweetie' I mean high value dog treat, not liquorice all-sorts or jelly babies sweets... something that really does it for your puppy; a small piece of cocktail sausage, tiny piece of cheese or a morsel of chicken and so on.

And now, it really is time to roll up our sleeves and get down to the wonderful task of getting to grips with all things puppy, finding out about what makes him tick, how to 'talk' to him, train him, motivate him and most important of all... how to have a happy, healthy and balanced relationship with him. Enjoy...

Lez Graham.
Spring 2018

You want a *what?*

A puppy? Oh fantastic... or was it more a case of wearing down your other half until they said yes?

Either way, whether this is your first puppy, or you've had puppies in the past, bringing home a new puppy is always a bit of a shock to the system, and welcoming a puppy into your home is absolutely huge.

In terms of the amount of time they're going to take up initially, you can easily compare it to bringing home a new baby. Not only will you be thinking about them every waking moment, but you'll have to completely reschedule your diary and learn (at least for the first couple of weeks) to cope with sleep deprivation, as you get up at silly o'clock to get the toilet training well and truly established.

Once you've come to terms with the fact that you're going to be tripping over toys, standing in 'accidents' or 'little presents', finding chewed furniture, having soggy chewsticks stuck to the bottom of your bare feet, have dog beds in every room (downstairs), are going to be walking your dog every day, rain or shine, are going to be hoovering every day and picking up between two and four dog poo's a day... it's very exciting!

Before we start looking for a puppy though, presuming of course you haven't already put your name down for one or have one lying at your feet (or even better in their crate), you need to ask yourself the soul-searching question of why a dog? As opposed to, say, a cat?

If you can answer this question then finding the type of dog that will suit you will be so much easier; whether you want a lap dog or a big couch potato, want to do some exciting sports with them or a dog to keep you company while you go hill walking, there's a type of dog out there that will be a perfect match.

Once you have an answer to 'why', then you need to work out what's important to you as a dog owner... because dogs do come in all different shapes, sizes, colours and coat types as well as ear shapes, tail lengths and moult-ability. (Okay, it's not really a word... but it should be).

Whether it's the long curly-haired ears of the Cocker Spaniel or the upright funnels of the Boston Terrier, the feistiness of the Chihuahua or the regal elegance of the Borzoi, knowing what 'does it' aesthetically is a good place to start... there's no point at looking at a Bernese Mountain Dog if you like a short fuss-free coat, you'd be better off looking at the Swiss Mountain Dog instead which looks very similar but with less fur.

Then, we look for breeds that fit what we like and within those breeds we look at health concerns.

It may seem a bit back to front starting with looks, but one of the many reasons dogs appeal so much to us, is how they make us feel when we look at them, and if we love the look of our puppy and the dog he's going to grow into, then we'll be so much more inclined to bond with them quickly and put more effort in to training and walking them.

And I am speaking from experience; for me you simply can't beat the feel of massaging a silky-smooth Labrador's ear or sinking your hands into the full ruff of a Golden Retriever; and I'm saying that with the most fabulous black Working Cocker lying at my feet (as well as my young black lab).

Before you decide, if you haven't already, which breed of dog you would really like to share your life with, it's important to understand 'the dog'; what it is and where the various breed 'types' originated from...

Canis Lupus Familiaris a.k.a.
THE DOG

It means so many things to so many people; to some it invokes fear, to others it brings a wistful smile as they remember all of those that have shared their lives, and to some a chuckle or a knowing shake of the head and a roll of the eyes.

Whatever your initial reaction is, there's no getting away from it; the dog is as much a part of our society as it's ever been. Its place in it though has changed many times from a feared and scavenging predator, to dog of war, to guide dog for the blind, to lap dog... the dog has been there throughout our history, and as such, it is the history of the dog that this book starts with.

So just what is a dog and how has it become such an important part of our lives?

Why do our dogs behave the way that they do? Why are some breeds diggers, some chasers, while others are only interested in sniffing and hunting? And why do they want to bring things back? Why not settle down under a tree and enjoy the spoils of the chase or that decomposing bit of 'yuck' that they found under the bush?

To truly understand the answers to the questions above we need to look to the dog's history, before there were specific breeds, even before there were 'types' of dogs; yup, we need to go back to when our Canis Lupus Familiaris was still a Canis Lupus.

Because the skeleton of the early dog is so similar to that of the wolf, historians have found it incredibly difficult to put a time on when the wolf became part of our family; some say domestication started as far back as 120,000 years ago, however most historians agree that by 32,000 years ago the dog was recognised as a separate animal to the wolf.

From Nomads to Farmers

The presumption is, that at some point, no doubt when pickings were a bit lean, the wolf discovered man. It is believed that sometimes the braver wolf would steal pickings from the group, probably by rushing in the 'back door' while man was chasing other wolves from the front.

A lone wolf may have followed nomadic man as way of gaining an easy meal and perhaps man took pity on the animal, throwing it scraps and thereby sealing its loyalty to a new pack... only this time a pack of human hunters.

No doubt it wouldn't have taken man long to take advantage of the fact that there was not only another hunter in the group, but a superior hunter; faster, stealthier and a better tracker with excellent hearing, a superb nose and one that could see much better in the dark.

Early man had in effect been adopted by an animal that was superior in pretty much every way bar 'intelligence', that provided for the group and could warn of danger approaching much sooner than anyone else.

It is believed that without the wolf 'watching our backs', man wouldn't have had the time to turn his attention to things other than 'bringing home the bacon', and that this relationship had a significant part to play in man settling down for periods of time, rather than having a more nomadic existence.

Having a superior hunter in the family can only have been a good thing, not just from a hunting perspective but from a protection point of view also. There is a reason why ladies feel the need to go to the toilet in groups and it's a very instinctive reason; when you squat you are in an extremely vulnerable position and would need someone to watch your back. Think of all the time saved by that early man-wolf relationship of not having to have human sentries on "ladies' toilet duty"!

When howl became bark

All those tens of thousands of years ago, without realising what they were doing, early man started a breeding programme that forever changed the Wolf into the Dog. Any aggression towards man would have resulted in that wolf being removed from the gene pool and the pelt used for warmth, the bones for glue, hollow organs as containers and so on.

By doing this one act, man started a chain of events that slowly, but surely, created a sub species of the wolf that actively started to seek out the company of another species rather than its own.

In 1959, Russian scientists tried to recreate this domestication process using the silver fox (it's a well-documented experiment – just type 'silver fox domestication' into google).

By breeding the non-aggressive foxes to non-aggressive foxes, not only did the fox start to become tame and react in a positive and playful manner around people, but its coat colour changed from silver, to silver and white, and black and white.

For me though, the most significant and mind-blowing changes were that its tail started to curl and in some cases the ears started to flop; the tame silver fox was developing 'dog ears'!

It wasn't just the removal of aggression from the gene pool that had an impact on the evolution from wolf to dog, the environment would have played a big part as well.

The legs and back would have been longer on the dogs that lived on the plains so that they had the turn of speed to match and surpass the fast prey of the open ground; short legged short backed dogs for the wooded areas so that they could duck into the undergrowth and turn quickly; shaggy, well haired dogs for the cold climates and so on.

Tweaking and tinkering

Knowing the way that people are, we could quite easily romanticise and imagine early man, as he traded with villages and other communities, admiring and wanting some of the traits from 'the others' dogs.

Just like us they would no doubt have swapped stories and bragged about how their dog could scare off a bear, or a lion, or that it could hunt tirelessly for days on end. Who knows, perhaps the perfect timing of a community gathering combined with a bitch in heat helped to spread the genes (and the traits) north to south and east to west.

Breeding for what we needed in our dogs would have made the function that we used them for much easier, and so tweaking and tinkering, which is very much a human trait, would have ensued.

In fact the earliest books about hunting, The Art of Venery (1327) and The Boke of St Albans (a school book about hawking, hunting, fishing and heraldry, dated 1486) refers to the dog by the function that it performed, for example, Butchers Dogs, Levriers (Greyhounds), Limers (medieval scent hounds that were used on lead to find large game, thought to be the forerunner to the bloodhound), Spaniels, Ratters, Kennets (small hunting dogs believed to be a beagle or similar) and, my all-time favourite, 'the Small Ladies Puppies that bear away the fleas'.

The start of the lapdog perhaps?

Exploiting instincts

This early blossoming relationship between man and their wolf-like canid would have suited both species really well; man, because he is a social predator by nature, and the canid, because, well, that's a social predator too – both species living in family units and hunting in co-operative groups for the good of the group/family/pack.

In the same way that human hunters provided for their family so too would the dog's predecessor have provided for their pack; the youngsters would be left at the den area along with an allocated 'nanny' to ensure the youngsters were safe or didn't try to follow the hunt. The hunters would then return with meat; either by carrying it in their mouths, or, as was more common, in their stomachs, regurgitating it upon return or demand.

Just as 'the pack' is the be all and end all for the wolf, so too is it for 'the dog', more so for the early dog who would have been 'tame' but not domesticated.

Being part of a hunting party (rather than leading the hunt) would have tapped into the early wolf-like dogs' intrinsic behaviour of lead or follow, thereby ensuring that the kill was brought back to the leader, who, in both worlds, gets to choose whether they eat first or not.

It is this inherent behaviour of having to bring the spoils back and defer to the leader that made the dog such a good hunting companion.

What came first? Form or function?

As man's hunting prowess developed, with the help of his new hunting companion, he would have found ways of exploiting the dog's innate behaviours and as part of breeding for specialised skills, the look of the dog would have changed also.

Let's just say you lived in a forested area and wanted a dog that could help hunt in woodlands, you'd be looking for shorter legged short backed dogs and wouldn't be breeding from taller rangy dogs. Over a short space of time a 'look' would be established and as we bred for function, the conformation (form) would have followed, in turn 'feeding' the function.

Just by looking at the conformation of the modern dog, you can pretty much tell where it's strengths lie, for example, when a Bloodhound, or a Bassett Hound (think short legged version) puts its head down, the ears fall forward and create a funnel for the scent to go straight up the dog's nose, which is why they can become very 'blinkered' very quickly, as anything 'outside of the nose' ceases to exist, due to that small area, cordoned off by the ears, being so concentrated.

As a behaviourist I'm always surprised, although I shouldn't be, that people buy dogs because they're the fashionable 'Working Cocker' or a cute 'Jack Russell' and then rehome them because they have no recall due to hunting all the time (the spaniel) or barking non-stop (the terrier).

Well yes, we did actively breed them to hunt and we did actively breed them to bark – a silent Jack Russell working underground wouldn't last very long if it got stuck in a tunnel... Quiet Quentin would have been irrevocably and permanently removed from the gene pool.

Behold the modern dog

Whether breeding for function or breeding for form; the beginning has been the same - the grey wolf. Whether tweaking and tinkering with hunting ability, retrieving ability, speed, agility, steadiness, short coat, long coat or coat colour, the blueprint of instinctive behaviour is the same; a social predator that thrives in a hierarchical environment.

So how did we get from 'the Small Ladies Puppies that bear away the fleas', to Best in Show at Crufts?

Well in 2011 it was reported that Chavet cave in France had paintings of hunting and grazing animals going back 35,000 years, however, what really got the experts excited, was that in the back of the cave, there were footprints of a boy, alongside large, wolf-like paw prints dating back 26,000 years.

We already knew that our relationship with the dog went back, at the very least, to the last ice age as we migrated across the land bridge from Europe to the UK together, and that was believed to have separated around 8,500 years ago.

There have been doglike remains dated at 15,000 years old and a study was carried out in 1997 which dated the split from wolf to dog at 135,000 years ago. All a bit mind blowing, isn't it?

For me to get my head around the history of the amazing relationship we have with our dogs, without getting too deep, I tend to think wolf, wolf-like dogs, dogs, and the first image I can easily conjure in my mind is of the Romans with their mastiff-type dogs armoured up for war. It must have resonated with Shakespeare too as it is from his play 'Julius Caesar' that we get the saying "let slip the dogs of war".

And it wasn't just for battle that Caesar used dogs. Without the assistance of dogs to herd livestock around, the Roman army wouldn't have gotten very far as their time would have been spent on hunting rather than on conquering.

By the time we get to the Middle Ages the dog started to be classified by the job it did for us, whether that was the drover's dog, a ratter or the lady's puppy; their conformation, to a degree, would have dictated the role they played. The Deerhound for example would not have fitted on the lady's lap and the lap dog would not have been very successful at bringing down a deer.

There has always been a 'class' associated with the dog; in historic times, the sighthounds were for those born into nobility or persons of rank, as were the hunting dogs; the peasants however kept mastiffs. Although we think 'fighting dog' when we think of these massive mastiffs, they were known in Britain in the middle ages as Tiedogs as they were tied up during the day and released at night to keep the villages safe from predators.

It was during the Industrial Revolution that things really started to change in the world of dog breeds and breeding. Up until this point, certainly in the UK, your position in the social class system was pretty much decided at birth, as social status and wealth were inherited. During this period of invention and industry, people started to move through the class system, and change their social standing.

It was right at the end of the Industrial Revolution that the middle classes had their eye on the lofty heights (and privileges) of the upper class but simply didn't have the wealth to emulate the activities like driven shoots and breeding horses and gundogs; what they did have sufficient wealth and standing to do, was 'tinker' with their pet dogs.

Copying their very wealthy counterparts, the middle classes recreated the livestock fairs by showing off their dogs. Being a Geordie lass, one of the things that I find highly amusing is that the first recorded 'best dog' show took place in 1859 in a local pub in, of all places, Newcastle upon Tyne.

The Kennel Club was formed in 1873 with their first studbook being published in 1874. It does make me wonder if The Jockey Club, which was founded in 1750 by a group of 'gentlemen' and who organised races 'for horses the Property of the Noblemen and Gentlemen belonging to The Jockey Club', hadn't been quite so upper class and exclusive, whether The Kennel Club would have been called something else.

One other notable thing that happened during this period that had a massive impact on the lineage of the dog, was the passing of The Humane Act of 1835, which made the keeping of a pit, room, house or place for the fighting and baiting of dogs (and other animals) illegal. It was at this point in history that dog fighting went underground and the 'pit' bull terrier was born.

The way that we viewed our relationship with dogs changed so much during this period, it's quite jaw-dropping really; lap dog, working dog, scullery dog, show dog, guard dog, war dog, competition dog, fighting dog, companion dog... and it has stayed pretty much the same since.

We still have 'type' although they are categorised further into a plethora of breeds, including type within breed; the Cocker Spaniel and the Working Cocker Spaniel for example are different in every way other than the Kennel Club registration papers.

In current times however, there seems to be as much a backlash against pedigree dogs as there is against the class system, as we see 'types' returning in the form of the doodle dog.

The Conflicted Crossbreed

Although for the past decade or so I've been known for having pedigree gundogs, it hasn't always been so. My first two dogs were crossbreeds, the classic Heinz 57s; at a guess, I would have said Kym was Labrador x German Shepherd x Rottweiler x Whippet whereas Sabre, well, I wouldn't know where to start... a classic hairy brindle mutt with the most amazing ears.

Growing up in the North East of England, I can't remember seeing that many pedigree dogs; the ones that were popular were the Border Collie and the Staffordshire bull terrier, along with the German Shepherd Dog. Pretty much all of my friends either had, or walked, Heinz 57s. The key here being the '57' tag. There were no designer cross breeds, not a one.

Were they healthier? Possibly. Were they from puppy farms? No, they were generally from a friend's auntie's bitch who'd been caught by the local stud.

At the time of writing this book (Winter 2017), designer gundogs were starting to become 'old hat', the reign of the cockapoo, labradoodle, springador and goldendoodle was starting to give way to the designer handbag dog; the poodle hybrid.

Although hybrid is entirely the wrong term as it denotes the crossing of two species, it's been picked as the latest buzz word for these extortionately priced crossbreeds; and I do mean extortionately priced – you're looking to pay, at the very least, £600-£800+ for a puppy from a parent that you know nothing about. This really is a way of giving unscrupulous breeders and puppy farmers a money printing press.

However, it's not so much the handbag 'hybrid' that is causing behaviourists to hold our heads; it is the crossing of the big, powerful and mentally strong, independent breeds.

Primarily based around the Husky because of the appealing facial mask and stunning blue eyes, the husky cross is currently being seen as the latest money maker. However, they are being crossed with fighting breeds (Akitas, Pitbulls), guarding breeds (German Shepherd,

Rottweiler) and hunting breeds (Labradors, Golden Retrievers); while some of these mixes may work, and it's got to be said some of them are stunningly beautiful to look at, many are a Pandora's box waiting to be unleashed.

When we think that these animals are going into pet homes, many with first time dog owners, it's not surprising that behaviour problems ensue, and rescue centres end up turning dogs away.

A Husky, or a Husky cross, is not for the faint-hearted or the inexperienced dog owner, regardless of how cute or stunning they look.

The Rise of The Malinois

At this time of global terrorism and mass media (or should that be media hysteria) a new phenomenon has taken a hold on social media, and I really do fear, as a behaviourist, the backlash.

What am I talking about I hear you ask? The war dog.

As we see the most amazing footage of Malinois' leaping out of helicopters, into moving cars, through burning hoops and being parachuted into action on the frontline, more and more people are wanting one of these dogs.

It's a bad idea. A very bad idea. They are not known as the Malligators for nothing. They tend to go at everything at a hundred miles an hour and when they bite they bite hard. They are difficult to live with as they're so full on; fantastic working dogs but they need to be trained, trained and trained some more to drain that amazing brain... and then, after a little rest they'll be back at you wanting more.

It was when I heard them described as 'German Shepherds on Speed' that I decided to include a little something here about them; as the owner of an incredibly fizzy working cocker spaniel that was named Spud after the speed taking character in the film Trainspotting, I understand just how difficult it can be to live with an over the top dog – and Spud only weighs 40lbs and measures 19 inches at the shoulder, the Malinois however can measure up to 24 inches at the shoulder and weigh up to 60lbs.

They are awesome dogs, handsome, intelligent and very much the Lamborghini of the dog world, however, before you start daydreaming about getting one, ask yourself this; would you really want to drive a Lamborghini every time you needed to go out in your car?

I know my husband would say yes, but just think of the palaver of speed bumps, steep ramps, narrow parking spaces and constantly having to keep the car in check when you can feel all that power waiting to be unleashed and not being allowed... with a dog you would also have to add into the mix free thinking and predatory response; definitely not for the faint-hearted or the inexperienced!

I can still remember the fallout following on from Disney's 101 Dalmatian's and Cats and Dogs. The Dalmatian and Beagle rescue centres were full to bursting within 18 months of the films being released as people bought these delightfully cute and playful puppies, only to realise what they'd brought home as the dogs started to grow up and hit adolescence... please, let's not make the same mistake with the Malligator.

The Malinois: one of the many Dogs of War.

Cairo, the dog that was so famously dropped from a helicopter and went on to find Osma Bin-Laden, is a Malinois.

Heinz '57, Designer or Pedigree?

Although some breeds are classed as being more intelligent than others, just like with humans, individuals learn at their own pace.

Generally speaking, the larger the breed the slower they are to mature, which does have an impact on their learning ability; the 'working types' do tend to be quicker on the uptake which isn't always a good thing as they need more mental stimulation, and so the tendency is to over exercise when young, meaning the levels of exercise they need as an adult is phenomenal as you end up with not only mentally alert dog but a physically fit one too.

Which breed to bring home is a major decision and one that needs to be taken by the adults in the family, not the children; I once recommended the rehoming of a 12-week-old Bernese Mountain Dog, as not only was it very inbred with 'issues' but it was totally unsuitable for the family. Why did they choose this breed? Because their four-year-old daughter wanted one to go with the fluffy toy one that she took everywhere with her! Need I say any more?

The choice, as they say, is yours... however to start you along the path to finding your perfect match, here's a summary of the breed groups as defined by the British Kennel Club; then Google really will be your friend to help you narrow the breed down within the group or give you an idea of what the various 'designer' dogs look like.

And remember, once you've chosen your breed, please look at the health issues prevalent in the breed, the temperament and care required and then be flexible enough to take a sideways step if necessary.

Gundog

The Gundog group consists of breeds of dogs that were originally trained to find live game and/or to retrieve game that had been shot and wounded. Although bred to work, they make good companions, their temperament making them ideal all-round family dogs.

The gundog group is the only group that is broken down into the sub-group of Retrievers (dogs that are bred primarily for retrieving; Labradors and Goldens being the most popular of the pet breeds), Spaniels (mainly hunting dogs; the Working Cocker Spaniel has become an incredibly popular pet thanks to the Duke and Duchess of Cambridge); Hunt Point Retrieve (also known as HPRs, these tend to be European breeds, the most popular being the German Short-haired Pointer, the Weimaraner and the Viszla) and finally the Pointers and Setters (which are primarily the British breeds, English Pointer, Irish Setter, Gordon Setter to name but three).

Hound

The Hound group consists of breeds that were originally used for hunting by either scent or sight. While the hound can be a good companion, they do need a lot of training and, as you might guess, they very quickly pick up the chase; only consistent and persistent training of this group will ensure a recall good enough for the dog to be allowed to run free.

The dogs that you'll find in the Hound group are Beagles, Bassets, Whippets, Greyhounds, Bloodhounds and the like.

Pastoral

The Pastoral group consists purely of herding dogs that are associated with working cattle, sheep, reindeer and other cloven- footed animals.

This is another group that is made up primarily from working breeds; Collies, Shepherds, Mountain Dogs and Cattle Dogs. All stunningly handsome breeds that need a lot of mental stimulation to satisfy the working brain.

Terrier

The Terrier group consists of dogs that were originally bred and used for hunting vermin. This hardy collection of dogs, were selectively bred to be extremely brave and tough, and to pursue fox, badger, rat and otter amongst others.

The most tenacious of all the dog breeds, terriers can make fabulous pets and they really do come in all shapes, sizes, coat type and colour; be aware though, that some of the breeds can be a bit on the barky side.

To make life easy, this group, unlike the others, all have the word Terrier in their breed name; Border Terrier, Welsh Terrier, Staffordshire Bull Terrier, Norfolk Terrier and so on....

Toy

The Toy group consists of small companion or lap dogs which were bred for this capacity and although the breeds in this group are small, they are only small in stature. They tend to have larger than life personalities and can be quite feisty little things at times.

The Cavalier King Charles Spaniel, the Chihuahua, Pug, Papillon and Pomeranian are all really popular toy breeds.

Utility

The Utility group consists of miscellaneous breeds of dog mainly of a non-sporting origin; an extremely mixed and varied bunch, most breeds having been selectively bred to perform a specific function not included in the sporting and working categories. Some of the breeds listed in this group are amongst the oldest documented breeds.

For me this group is 'I don't know where to put this breed, so I'll put it in the Utility group' and contains a vast range of sizes and temperaments, from the tiny toy Poodle (yes, I know, why isn't it in the toy group?) to the endurance paced Dalmatian, the small Lhasa Apso to the Japanese fighting dog, The Akita.

Working

Finally, the Working group consists of breeds that have, over the centuries, been selectively bred to become guards and search and rescue dogs. The Kennel Club describes them as the 'real specialists in their field who excel in their line of work', which I found quite interesting as pretty much all of the breed groups, with the exception of the toy, have breeds which are actively bred for working.

This group includes a great variety of breeds including the Boxer, the Doberman, the Mastiff, the Rottweiler and the Russian Black Terrier.

The Top Ten

In 2017 the ten most popular dog breeds in the UK were...

1. Labrador Retriever – Gundog
2. French Bulldog – Utility
3. Cocker Spaniel – Gundog
4. Pug – Toy
5. English Springer Spaniel – Gundog
6. Bulldog – Utility
7. Golden Retriever – Gundog
8. German Shepherd Dog – Pastoral
9. Miniature Smooth-Haired Dachshund – Hound
10. Miniature Schnauzer – Utility

And in 2016 the list looked like...

1. Labrador Retriever – Gundog
2. Cocker Spaniel – Gundog
3. French Bulldog – Utility
4. Pug – Toy
5. English Springer Spaniel – Gundog
6. Bulldog – Utility
7. German Shepherd Dog – Pastoral
8. Golden Retriever – Gundog
9. Miniature Schnauzer – Utility
10. Border Terrier – Terrier

The same top ten breeds as far as popularity goes, only in a slightly different order with the smaller breeds becoming slightly more popular in 2017.

It will be interesting to see if our love affair with the gundog, and in particular, the Labrador Retriever, wanes over the next couple of years as the French Bulldog gets ever more popular...

And how would the list have looked if the trendy designer crossbreeds and doodle dogs had been included?

Pick a breeder, any breeder...

Once you've decided on the breed or type of dog that you want, and you're happy that it will be suitable for your lifestyle, then the mammoth task of finding one that fits you and your family is underway.

Acquiring a puppy way back when was much easier than it is now; you knew someone who had a litter, or you knew someone whose mate had had a litter. My first dog came from my sister's dog, my second I rescued as a puppy from a family who couldn't toilet train him and so he was going to get put to sleep (as was the 'done' thing back in the day); next it was my first pedigree – Bart, a black Labrador.

I had absolutely no intention of getting a pedigree dog as I'd always loved the little black and tan crossbreeds that I grew up with, however, I fell in love with Bart's half-brother after he fell asleep on my lap on the way to a horse show and that was me hooked. I then went on a quest to get the same or similar breeding and found the most amazing breeder, Jill Stagg.

When it came time for me to get another puppy I was living in New Zealand and a client recommended a litter of Golden Retrievers which is where I got Angus from.

I returned to Jill for Ziggy, Bart's nephew; Spud my black Working Cocker was recommended to me by my vet and came to me when he was four months old as the gamekeeper who bred him didn't have time to train him for trialling, and finally, I went back to Jill for Ziggy's nephew, the magnificent Dante.

All very straight forward but what if I hadn't fallen in love with Barney, the little black Labrador puppy who snuggled on my lap in the horsebox? How would I have found a dog once we'd decided that we were going to have one?

Well, the best place to start is always word of mouth recommendation, either by seeing a friend's dog and liking the temperament or hearing about a dog from a friend or talking to the local vet to enquire about any litters from nice bitches that they know of.

A warning about falling in love with breeds that you see doing demonstrations at game fairs or dog shows. For the most part they are kennelled dogs, trained by extremely experienced trainers and have had two to three years training; they did not arrive trained, a lot of hard work has gone into them – a silly warning perhaps but I've seen many dogs rehomed after owners expected them to be at the same level as the game fair dogs after six months!

The Kennel Club website (see useful contacts) provides vast amounts of information for people looking to buy pedigree puppies. By typing in the breed that you're interested in, you are able to choose from breeders in your area by clicking on regions of a map; you can then read about litters that have been registered with the Kennel Club and when they'll be available.

The Kennel Club also operate The Assured Breeder Scheme which is about promoting good breeding practices; remember though that just because a breeder isn't part of this scheme doesn't mean they're not good and responsible breeders, it just means that they're not a member of the scheme.

Another great source of information for pedigree puppies are the breed clubs. I always recommend that you contact at least three breeders, and as well as asking them about their breeding lines, ask them about the other breeders that you may be interested in; you may just get a fuller picture.

Although I know lots of very good pedigree dogs that aren't registered with the Kennel Club, personally I would be wary of getting a pedigree that isn't KC registered. Why go to the expense of purchasing a pedigree dog without that final piece of paper?

There may come a time, further down the line, that you want to do an activity with your dog but in order to participate in it, your dog has to be a pedigree on the Kennel Club register. I've seen it time and again in my classes and always really feel it for my clients; if you're buying a pedigree dog, insist on registration.

Puppy farming is rife, dealing with pedigrees and the new designer cross-breeds, Cocker Spaniel x Poodle (the cockapoo), Pug x Beagle (the puggle), Maltese x Poodle (the maltipoo), and so on. Unfortunately, they're very canny and come up with all sorts of tricks to lead the trusting public astray... and the excuses are plenty – "oh my wife has just taken the mum out for a walk"; "oh she gets a little bit nervous around strangers"; "I can't find the photo of the sire – must have mislaid it"; "take two puppies as one on its own will be lonely"; "I only have two puppies left and it's not fair to only take one".

Absolutely insist on seeing the dam, with her puppies and stroke them around her. If you're getting a pedigree then ask to see a copy of both the dam's and the sire's pedigree papers and at the very least a photograph of the sire, preferably with the owner and preferably with the dam so at least you know there's a chance that they got together at some point.

Dogs do get sick in their lifetime and many factors contribute to the wellness of a dog – it's not always down to breeding, just like with us it can be down to lifestyle and diet.

However, *it is imperative* that the dam and sire (mam and dad) have been health screened according to what is prevalent in that breed, for example with Spaniels it's hips and eyes; Labradors it's hips, elbows and eyes. If you're going for a designer cross-breed then check that both parents have had the health screening done prevalent for that breed, so with the 'cockapoo' it would be hips and eyes for the Cocker and eyes for the Poodle.

The Kennel Club website has health information for each breed, including which health tests are mandatory for the pedigree dog to be registered, and although running the tests on the parents is no guarantee that your new puppy won't have any problems, you at least know he's got the best chance of having a clean bill of health.

Hopefully you're now at the stage where you have a list of breeders to phone, which will be quickly reduced down to a list of breeders to go visit alongside a list of questions ranging from 'has she had a litter before? Did you keep any of the puppies? Can I see them?', 'will the puppies be Kennel Club registered?', 'will their tails be docked (if working spaniels)?' all the way through to 'can I give one a cuddle?', some you will want to ask over the phone, others you'll want to ask before you see the puppies, while you're with the puppies and when you get home.

Now I know this is really easy to say, and much harder to do, but don't be pressured to making a decision there and then, especially in the times of the mobile phone; have a think about it and then give the breeder a ring – even if it's just five minutes down the road... just giving yourself a few minutes away from those adorable puppy eyes and intoxicating puppy smells will help.

Please, please, please... take a deep breath and walk away from the following; dirty kennels, unkempt dirty looking bitch, growly bitch, bitch not in attendance with puppies, breeder arranging to meet up at service stations and having puppies in the back (with or without bitch as this will likely be a puppy farmer), 2-3 other unrelated breeders advising against the line, hereditary diseases, aggression within the line and lack of health checks; it may save you years of heart ache.

Try not to take a puppy because you feel sorry for either the puppies or the bitch; I've seen puppies that have been put to sleep after a couple of months of absolute heart-ache for the families where they've taken a runty looking puppy because it's pulled at their heart strings...

However, do bear in mind, that the bitch will be feeding the puppies solely until the breeder helps by supplementing food at around the three to four-week mark, so if you visit around this time the bitch may look a bit on the slim side, especially if it's a large litter.

Arrange to visit again a couple of weeks later and her condition should have seriously improved; if it hasn't then walk away, go back to your list and resume your puppy hunt.

Decisions, Decisions...

So, you've found your breeder, they tick all the boxes for you and you tick all the boxes for them, you love the mum and the pups are adorable; you now have the unenviable task of choosing your puppy!

Where to start? Well if you have your heart set on a certain sex that rules out the some of the litter straight away. What about colour? Is colour important? If you want a black boy and there's only one then that's it, job done, but what if there's seven black boys to choose from?

If you're with a breeder that is giving you a choice on puppy ask if they can remove any of the puppies that do not 'fit the bill' so that you don't feel overwhelmed by all of the little bodies wriggling around; you'll find it much easier, especially if it's a large litter.

Although there are ways of testing to see if puppies are suitable for the home they're going to, my advice is, and always will be, give the breeder a list of what you're looking for in your dog and let the breeder choose for you. Why?

Well what you see on your visits (and you should visit more than once) are little snapshots into your puppy's life. You might be looking for a quiet little chap and think that the docile puppy, snoozing over there with his mates is perfect for you, much more suitable than the one that is trying to pull your laces to bits.

However, that docile puppy might, five minutes earlier, have been terrorising all the other puppies and has fallen asleep out of exhaustion, whereas the one chewing your laces has just woken up, is feeling good and is up for a little adventure before he has another wee snooze.

Your breeder however, will be spending any spare time they have looking after the puppies, fussing over them and generally hanging out with them and the dam and will know all their personalities. By the time the puppies are four or five weeks old, the breeder will have a good idea of what kind of dog the puppy will turn into and what family they'd be more suited to.

Remember though that you want your breeder to choose the potential dog for you and your family not for themselves; if the breeder competes or works their dogs and says, "if it was me I would have that one", then unless you're going to do some serious work with your dog, it would probably be best for the breeder to keep him and you take his 'number two', or even 'number three' on the list.

The Golden Retriever.

A strong but soft breed, the Golden Retriever endears himself to everyone he meets with his calm, lovable nature and open, expressive face.

Puppies 101

Before we get down to the nitty gritty of preparing your home for the arrival of your new family member, it's time for a quick overview of all things puppies.

Hopefully it will help you understand the various stages your puppy has been through since he was born and what he is going to go through over the next few weeks...

In the beginning

Your puppy, along with his siblings, will have been snuggled away inside of mum for around 63 days or 9 weeks. The dam (mum) will whelp (give birth) to between one and potentially upwards of 13 puppies, depending upon breed, although they won't really look like puppies – more like little moles.

Their eyes will be closed, their tiny little ear flaps will be sealed shut, their nervous system won't be fully developed, and they won't be able to control their own temperatures (or their bowels). In fact, the only thing that will be remotely working for these little creatures will be their noses, which within a few days, will be processing all 220 million scent receptors.

Once born, mum will clean them extensively, covering them with her scent; she'll also lick her nipples regularly too, not just to keep them clean but to leave a little scent trail for her puppies to follow, ensuring that they know the way to the 'milk bar'.

A new-born puppy can't move much at all and shuffles about using his head as a pendulum trying to locate mum and his litter mates; if he heads off too much in the wrong direction mum will either pick him up and bring him back or flip him over using her nose to push him back with his litter.

As you might guess the puppies don't really do much at first other than sleep, eat and grow. However, it all starts to change at around ten to fifteen days when the eyes begin to open; it's also around this time that the ear flaps start to lift and sounds, albeit quite muffled, are starting to be heard.

The Transition Period: weeks two and three

These two weeks are such an important and busy time for the little puppy; not only is he starting to see and hear but he's also starting to feel.

His temperature is starting to regulate itself, so he'll start dragging himself away from the litter using his front legs, which he'll have discovered are starting to work, however, more often than not, he'll find himself going backwards at this early stage; he'll also start to sit as he pushes his front end up leaving his rear behind.

It's towards the end of this period that the eyes open fully although it won't be until weeks four to six that they can more or less see what an adult dog sees, and it will be another week or so after that, before the eyes start to change from a milky blue towards the colour that they will be as an adult.

The ears also open fully during this time, although in pricked ear breeds it will be a couple of months before the pinna is strong enough to stand up.

As with the eyes, the hearing won't be as defined as an adult dog's until around four to six weeks and then it will take another couple of months for the puppy to learn to be discerning in relation to sound.

The Socialisation Period: weeks three/four to twelve

The Socialisation Period is also known as the 'critical period in your puppy's growth' and stretches from weeks three/four to week twelve of your puppy's life; as you might guess from the name that has been given to it, it's all about socialisation.

There is a bit of an overlap between the transition period and the socialisation period, which is known as the awareness period or the period of awareness, and is from days 21 to 28.

The change in sensory awareness happens very quickly for the puppy, more or less overnight, and that is when the puppy becomes aware of his surroundings, his mum and his litter mates; it's also a time when he needs his litter and the familiar surroundings the most. As you can imagine this is the worst possible time for him to be taken away from the litter or for the litter as a group to be moved.

The socialisation period is split into two distinct learning phases; the first is about socialisation with their own species and learning all about how to be a dog, the second phase is about socialisation beyond their species... that means us!

Canine Socialisation: weeks three to seven

Between three and seven weeks the puppy learns all about being a dog and he learns it from his mum and his siblings.

Once he has all of his communication 'gear' in working order it's time to learn how to communicate; this involves using facial expression as well as body language, ear positioning and tail wags.

It really is quite comical to watch five-week-old puppies strutting their stuff, heads held high, ears flattened whilst their erect little tails are wagging away – all very important stuff as they learn how to communicate through posture and, just as importantly, learn to read it in their litter mates.

As well as learning all the 'posturing stuff', these little puppies have to learn what it feels like to bark at another dog and in turn be barked at; they also have to learn how to bite and be bitten. You'll not believe the noise that comes out of the puppies' box from four weeks or so; growls, barks, yips, yaps and screams.

My breeder always has a little camera in the box with them and keeps the monitor with her; sitting having a coffee when there's puppies around is amazing – you just can't take your eyes off the screen, watching the little souls interact with each other, playing pounce and chase and bite and "ouch you play too hard"... seeing it in action and watching the behaviours unfold naturally is just fantastic.

It is during this time that the young puppy learns about pack hierarchy and his place within it; oh, and he also learns about discipline... discipline from his mum and discipline from his litter mates.

From his siblings, he learns to dominate or show deference; to climb over or be climbed upon. He also learns how much pressure he can apply with his little jaw... too much will cause a softer puppy to scream and not play any more whereas too much with a stronger puppy will leave him open to be attacked, thereby learning not only how to play nice but also how to show deference to a senior rank to prevent aggression.

His mum will discipline him either by using a paw to pin him in place or a low growl to let him know he's gone too far, especially when she's starting to wean them off the teat; if he really pushes his luck she may air snap at him although there'll be massive amounts of facial expression first; furrowed brow, hard stare, a wrinkling of the nose as well as a general bristling and freezing of the body... all important lessons in canine communication.

At around week four, or thereabouts, depending on litter size and condition of the mum, the breeder will start to introduce a bit of 'mush' to help supplement mum's milk; this is the beginning of the weaning process and of mum starting to distance herself from her puppies.

It is around this time when the whelping bitch generally looks at her worst as most of the nutrients from her food have gone into producing milk; no more though, once the breeder starts to help out with a bit of mush, mum will start to be able to put on condition again.

Human Socialisation: weeks seven to twelve

Between seven and twelve weeks is when the puppy learns how to interact with people, learning about us in the way that he learned about his litter; how to read our facial expressions, our body language and our energy.

He has to learn about our world; about carpets and lino, TVs and radios, aerosol sprays, hoovers, flushing toilets... the list really is endless, and he has to be exposed to it all. However, there is one massive thing that is working against us as we bring our puppy home – the fear impact period which runs from weeks eight to eleven.

The puppy's first reaction to many things at this point can be fear and it's up to us as their leader and protector to make things less scary; that doesn't mean we mollycoddle and soothe our puppies, it just means putting a bit of forethought and common sense into introducing our puppies to something new.

Bye Mum

The most common time for puppies to leave the litter is between seven and nine weeks; before this time and the puppy will miss out on valuable lessons from his litter mates on how to behave, especially in relation to biting.

When it's left until 12 or 13 weeks, you'll be bringing home a puppy right in the middle of the first fear period which, if he hasn't been socialised effectively during the extra weeks by his breeder, can find it harder to adapt to life with you and yours and can be on the nervy side because of it.

Bear in mind that each puppy is an individual and so the start and end 'dates', if you like, of each phase in their life is fluid by a few days.

Hopefully after working your way through the early stages of a puppy's development, you'll understand why singleton puppies are such hard work and why I would only recommend them to a very experienced puppy owner.

Likewise, why bringing home two puppies from the same litter is such a bad idea; one will always be a more senior rank and discipline the other, and if it's not checked by a strong leader (us) can lead to out and out bullying making both dogs lives miserable in the process.

The first Fear Period

Your puppy's first fear period or fear impact period as it's more commonly, or technically known, occurs between weeks eight and eleven, just as you're bringing your puppy home. Anything that is traumatic or scary or sometimes just big, bold and noisy can have a lasting effect, however it doesn't have to.

Let's just say for example a tray falls on the floor and your puppy scoots off down the hall... your first reaction may be to baby him "there-there baby, it's just a tray falling on the floor, nothing to worry about" and you may carry him back and give him a cuddle.

Alternatively, it might look so funny that you can't help but laugh, even as you're going towards him to reassure him that it's okay.

Alternatively, you could do nothing other than walk over to the tray pick it up and carry on doing what you were doing.

The last one, believe it or not, is the way to react; the first two are praising the reaction, in this case fear, confirming that when your puppy hears a loud and unexpected noise the correct response should be fear and running away.

Remember you cannot reason with a puppy, or with a dog for that matter, and reassurance, cooing over and fussing all count as praise in your dog's eyes and when does your dog get praised? When he's doing the right thing.

It is also during this first fear period that your puppy will visit the vets for his welcome home health check and, if you're vaccinating, then for his first vaccination.

Please do your puppy a favour and make them separate visits so that the first time your puppy gets to go to the vets it's a nice experience for him and he'll associate the smell of disinfectant with strokes, smiles, treats and good things happening.

Seniority Classification Period: weeks twelve to sixteen

At around twelve to thirteen weeks your puppy will be moving into another stage of his development which will last until he is sixteen weeks of age and moving out of puppyhood and into adolescence.

This is called the Seniority Classification period and is all about your puppy learning about leadership and where he fits within the pack, what the boundaries are, what he can get away with and what he can't.

It doesn't happen overnight, rather it's a build up over four or five weeks and for most puppy owners it's a time of frustration; they feel as if their cuddly little ball of fluff is deliberately doing something to 'wind them up', whether that's running away from them in the garden or chewing anything and everything the second their backs are turned.

Take heart, they're really not; just like with a child starting school, your puppy is checking the boundaries and testing that they still hold true now that he's starting to 'grow up'.

Your puppy is going to go through some serious changes physically as well as psychologically. You'll probably notice that at times he doesn't look quite so level at the shoulder and the back end as the growth spurts tend to make puppy grow back end, front end, back end, front end and at some point, in the front end growing, the baby teeth start to get pushed out and some serious teething occurs.

Now is the time to invest in some hard-plastic teething toys, keep them in the fridge so that they're nice and cooling to your puppy's hot gums and make sure you always leave one in the crate for him to give him some relief when he needs it.

If you're into homeopathic remedies then Nelson's Teetha, designed for teething children, can help your puppy through this stage if it bothers him; like with children losing their baby teeth some go through with no discomfort whereas with others it's a bit of a painful drawn out process.

Not surprisingly, this period of growth is also known as The Age of Cutting and is not only the time that the puppy cuts his adult teeth, but also the time of cutting the apron strings... it heralds the end of being puppy and launches your dog into adolescence.

Although we tend to call our puppies 'puppy' until they're about a year old, physically and psychologically, it is around weeks 16-20 that they are a puppy no more...

The Basset Hound.

The Basset Hound is a slow and steady tracking dog. While short and solid in stature, the Basset should have good ground clearance and be athletic enough in build to be able to steadily track over many miles a day of rough and uneven ground and thick undergrowth.

The Final Countdown

Feeling prepared for your puppy's arrival is the key to keeping the event exciting rather than stressful, or should that say keeping the stress levels to a minimum.

Your home

One of the most effective ways to puppy-proof your home is to invest in a crate: and I said 'crate', not 'cage'. Many people are put off getting crates for their puppy as in their mind they read 'cage', but trust me, it is the easiest way not only to puppy-proof your home but to toilet train – and to keep your sanity.

Try to get a smaller crate to start off with as if it's too large your puppy may want to use one end as a toilet, so either get a smaller cheap crate to start off with or invest in one that comes with a divider that you can move as the puppy grows.

Place your crate in the room that you're likely to be in most once the puppy arrives and try to place it fairly close to the 'toileting' door. If your kitchen is big enough this tends to be the best place, or the utility room if you have one, or the dining room, or, if you work from home, your office providing it's near an outside door, otherwise consider temporarily moving your office... as you might have guessed, the room the crate is in isn't important but the locality to an outside door is.

Drape a single bed sheet over the crate so that it can cover the top and three sides down to the ground. If you can match it with the colour of the room it will blend in, look more like it belongs rather than a 'cage'.

Not only will you feel more comfortable putting your puppy in it, but, more importantly, it will feel like a den to the puppy, which, if left to their own devices, is where the mum would have wanted to have given birth.

You may want to put an old towel or a bit of carpet under the crate to protect the carpet that it's going to be on, or, if your crate is going on lino, laminate or tiles, pop a bit of carpet under it pile side down, as it will make it much easier to move the crate around for cleaning the floor.

Walk around the rooms and check that there are no trailing cables or anything sticking up that the puppy may find super interesting; if your carpet has started to come up from the skirting or the runner, now is the time to fix it as I guarantee that if you don't your puppy 'will'.

Now, get down on your hands and knees and look at the rooms from your puppy's perspective; it looks very different, doesn't it?

Your garden

Take a walk around the garden and look for any gaps in hedges and fences and attach chicken wire to the bottom of gates and if needed below the fence; you'll be amazed what your puppy can squeeze through and under when you take your eyes off him for a minute.

Google 'poisonous plants for dogs' and you'll get a comprehensive list, not only that, it means your list is always up to date, unlike a book which is out of date the second it is sent to the printers; if you don't have a computer at home then pop down to the local library and ask the librarian to help you do this - if my memory serves right it will only cost the price of a standard photocopy or it may even be a donation for the printing cost.

Do you have steps and walls? I remember when Angus was a puppy, we had a drop down into the garden of about 12 inches and he would want to leap off it like a polar bear launching itself off an ice floe; he thought it was great fun, and it was, but it didn't stop my heart leaping into my mouth whenever he did it.

Try as I might, the second he got the chance he was going for it, in the end I stopped trying to stop him and just monitored the amount of time he was in the back garden until he was 4 months old.

A single step isn't so bad providing that, unlike Angus, they don't launch themselves off it, and that they are landing on a soft surface, however, multiple steps are dangerous; not only will they be hard landing but the repeated bounce, bounce, bounce down them will jar your puppy's little elbow joints which is something to be avoided at all costs.

Also, a young puppy hasn't got the greatest co-ordination and sense of balance, so may end up putting too much weight over their front end and topple tail over head down them.

If you have steps in your garden cordon them off until your puppy is older and more in control; in terms of co-ordination, basic obedience and good manners.

Do you have a pond? If so cover it up and fence around it; try to treat the arrival of your puppy as you would the arrival of a toddler or a baby that is crawling – into everything and everything into their mouth, so as you're inspecting your garden (and your home) try to think toddler-proof as well as puppy-proof.

Your car

Safety in the car is so important, not only for your puppy but for us also, and, apart from the journey home which I always recommend is on a passenger's lap, the best way for a puppy to travel is in a crate.

Not only will the crate keep your puppy safe in the event of an accident, but it will stop him from being thrown around the car at speed when you go around bends; it will also keep your car intact when you leave your puppy in it. As your puppy gets older you may want to invest in a dog guard/tail gate but initially you just cannot beat a crate.

Your shopping lists

There are so many things available for the new puppy and even more ways of bending the new puppy owner's 'plastic'... manufacturers just keep coming up with new ways of enticing people to spend money, so here is my list of essential puppy items; hopefully not too bank breaking!

- 2 crates, one for the car and one for the home. They should be big enough for your puppy to lie flat and stand up along with a little bit of growth space. Don't make them too big though as your puppy may decide to sleep at one end and toilet in the other.
- A crate bowl (also known as a coup cup) so that puppy can move around without spilling the water
- 2 metal puppy food bowls
- Puppy collar and lead (cheap set, your puppy will grow out of the collar very quickly)
- 2 soft toys
- 2 medium chewing toys
- 2 robust chewing toys
- 2 Puppy kongs
- 3 Vet beds per crate (one spare, one in the wash and one in the crate)
- Toy box that has a lid

Split the toys and put half in the box and put them away, that way you'll be able to rotate the toys to stop puppy getting bored and will save you spending an absolute fortune on toys.

Keep the kongs out of the toy boxes though and use them instead in the crate to help settle your puppy.... more on this later.

Your Self

And finally, You.... Are you ready for this?

Have you booked out the next couple of weeks to settle puppy and toilet train. You should really be looking on the new arrival as, well, a new arrival. You're going to be absolutely shattered and will only really be able to do anything when your puppy's in his crate, which will seem like an awful lot but still won't be enough to get everything done.

If you've had puppies before then you kind of know what you're letting yourself in for, although no two puppies are the same and we humans are great at looking at the past through rose tinted glasses... every single person I know who gets a puppy always say that they forget how much hard work and time consuming it is in the early days.

You literally won't have time to turn around let alone socialise – be prepared to put your life on hold for 2-3 weeks after the puppy comes home as you'll be shattered.

Honestly, I'm not exaggerating – think of it as bringing home a new baby; just a new baby of a different species who hasn't got a clue as to what's going on, is in an alien world, is very, very dependent on you and whom you cannot take your eyes off for a minute.

Mentally you need to prepare for the responsibility that dog ownership entails. Remember that when you take on a dog it really is for life, or at least that's how it should be approached.

You will need to make all of the decisions for your puppy and, as he matures, for your dog. One of the biggest responsibilities for a dog owner is sticking to the unspoken bond between you and the puppy that you bring home that you will always do your best by them, that you will not let them suffer unnecessarily, and that you will be brave enough to make that final appointment at the vets in a timely manner when the need arises... timely, that is, for your dog, not for you.

The Border Terrier.

Essentially a working terrier from The Borders region of Scotland and England, this little dog has a great character and bags of energy. As well as being a superb ratter, the border terrier makes a fabulous agility dog.

Bringing your puppy home

When you go to collect your new puppy, go armed with poo bags, kitchen roll and a towel... and possibly some water depending upon how long you're going to be in the car for.

The journey home is a fantastic time to bond with your puppy and this is the one and only time that I recommend that your puppy is on your lap as opposed to in his crate. Whoever is going to be the puppy's owner should be the person to cuddle puppy on the way home, that way the puppy will be covered in their scent and will associate that person with the first safe haven upon leaving the litter... so be patient with your little chap.

If you can make the journey last more than twenty minutes that would be perfect as it will give the puppy a chance to settle on your lap; if it's a mammoth journey, then crate your puppy to give you both a bit of peace but have a stop for a cuddle if possible without taking any chances in relation to safety.

Remember not to make a drama out of any accidents that happen on the way home, just calmly and quietly wrap it up in kitchen roll or, if you've got puppy on a towel, just fold the towel over it.

The way that I bring my puppies home is wrapped in a towel on my lap with kitchen roll to hand and a little chewy toy in case the puppy decides my hair is fair game.

I never wear perfume as I don't want my puppy's delicate nose getting overwhelmed with chemicals and I'd rather it recognised me and my scent, as opposed to the latest thing I spray on my wrists.

Settling him in

So, you've got your puppy home, what's next?

If the weather allows, hang out in the garden with your puppy for a little while, offer him a drink and a little food (although with all of the excitement it's unlikely he'll want to eat). Once your puppy has stretched his legs encourage him into your home, just the room where his crate is for now, ensuring all the other doors are closed.

It's a good idea to make this one room your puppy's world for the next week to give him a chance to learn a routine and feel safe in his new environment. He's gone through a massive upheaval leaving his mum and his litter mates so keeping everything calm at home this week is really important as we don't want to completely overwhelm him.

Settle yourself on the floor and just watch your puppy. It's this quiet time of 'just being' that will help you bond with each other and because you're being quiet and letting your puppy explore you're demonstrating strong, quiet leadership (which your puppy needs) without fussing which can excite a young puppy.

Keep an eye out for any tell-tale signs of your puppy needing the toilet, sniffing one place, circling or scratching... that's the time to turn on a bit of excitement and encourage your puppy out of the house and into the garden; you may have a little wait again but don't go back indoors until your puppy has 'performed'; if it's wet out or you're a bit worried about your puppy making it to the garden in time, pick him up and quietly carry him to the toileting area.

Toilet training

The only way to be successful in your toilet training is to be vigilant.

Your puppy has absolutely no concept at this moment in time what is acceptable to his new pack and what is unacceptable; the only way he is going to learn that is by you being vigilant and consistent in your approach.

You need to take your puppy to the designated toileting area every time he's eaten, had a drink, wakes up and after play, as well as any time you see him sniffing an area or circling. The more you catch this in the next few days the easier it will be to toilet train your puppy.

If you can, try to encourage him to follow you out to the garden rather than carry him, that way he'll learn the route quicker; also, if you pick him up you may make the 'urge to go' go away and then you'll have missed your chance.

To encourage your puppy to toilet in the same place in the garden, 'fluff' the grass with your fingers and make a sniffing noise as that will get your puppy over to the area and sniffing, then as he starts to toilet, repeat a 'toilet' word over and over.

What you're doing is classically conditioning him to want to toilet when he hears a certain word so think carefully about 'the word' before you start as you'll be using for it the next however many years when you want him to toilet on command. I use 'go toilet' and 'finish off' but have conditioned my dogs to 'toilet time' which is the cue for going in the garden.

Make a fuss of him for toileting in the garden, then make a game of dashing back indoors to his crate and pop him in it with a treat, as this will encourage him to get straight back indoors after toileting rather than messing around in the garden...

You can also give him another little treat once the crate door is closed if you wish and then let him out again, but build up the time between him going back in the crate and letting him out as more often than not he'll stay in the crate after toileting (when you go to work).

Make sure that you always use the same door to the garden for toileting so that your puppy knows which door to head to once he cottons on that he needs to go out to toilet. Once he starts indicating he needs to go by heading to the door you can start adding another command or prompt; mine is "Is it toilet time?" which quickly turns to "toilet time" once they're trained and I want them to go.

In the early days of crate training remove access to all water bowls (in or out of the crate) about two hours before bedtime, this will give him a chance to empty his tanks before bed and will encourage him to be dry overnight.

However, if it's very warm or you're feeding him dried food only, then offer him a little water half an hour before his last toilet break, remembering to offer him water first thing in the morning once he's been to the loo.

Once he's dry through the night, which should only take a week or so, then start allowing him a small amount of water in his crate overnight.

To speed up your toilet training it's a good idea to go to bed late and get up very early, so say bed around 11pm / midnight, and up at about 4am to let puppy out for the toilet; don't worry though you can go straight back to bed, especially if you don't make a fuss, do everything with dimmed lights and quiet voices.

If you add a quarter of an hour per night to the time you have to get up it won't take long for your puppy to be going from 10:30-11pm through til 6:30-7am.

Puppy Pads

I've seen quite a few clients who've had problems toilet training their puppy and are who are still experiencing their young dog toileting around the home well into adolescence. The common denominator in all the cases have been the trendy (and expensive) puppy pads.

The puppy pad was invented back in the 1970's by a carpet fitter turned dog groomer as a way of protecting the carpet from 'accidents'. They are scented to encourage the puppy to the right spot to toilet, thereby saving the carpet... a clever and money-making replacement for sheets of newspaper which were traditionally used when house training a puppy.

I've never been fond of house-training a puppy to paper and am even less enamoured with the thought of spending a fortune training a puppy on puppy pads...

At the end of the day, by using pads, or paper, you are training your puppy to toilet indoors, and toilet indoors whenever he feels like it. So not only are you rewarding the very behaviour you're trying to avoid but your puppy is not learning bladder and bowel control, and he's not learning that he needs to communicate to you when he needs to go outside.

There then comes a day when you forget to put down a pad or the puppy plays with it and the soiling begins... I can't stress enough that the only way to successfully house train your puppy is through vigilance and putting your life on hold for a couple of weeks,

Crate training

The key to crate training is to make the crate the best place in the world for the puppy... and that means food and toys!

Every meal that your puppy has should be fed in his crate; while he's eating close the crate door and build up the amount of time between him finishing eating and opening the door to let him out, but please bear in mind during the early days of toilet training, that eating stimulates your puppy to want to go to the toilet.

Your puppy should have his crate door closed overnight and initially, whenever you're out of the room as the last thing you want is to nip out of the room for five minutes and get back to a trashed room and a little 'present' in the middle of it, or, much worse, a puppy that has been injured or electrocuted due to chewing through a wire.

Feed your puppy all his meals in the crate so that he associates it with nice things happening. Invest in a couple of puppy kongs so that you can stuff them with his puppy food and then when you return your puppy back to his crate after toileting after a meal, you can give him a stuffed kong to help him settle down rather than a 'toileting' treat. Stuff it quite loosely to start off with and remember to reduce his meal allowance by the amount of food used in his kong.

I feed my dogs a raw diet, so I tend to firmly pack some of their food into a kong and freeze it until it starts to firm up and then give it to my puppy as I'm settling them in the crate for an hour. If you're not a raw feeder, then I would recommend using firm wet dog food that holds together when pressed into the kong.

As with the toileting routine, after the first day or so start to close the crate door when settling your puppy down with a kong.

When your puppy is tired encourage him into the crate with a food treat and help him to settle and sleep in the crate by sitting on the floor by the open door and stroke him until he nods off, then quietly close the door, without locking it.

Again, after a couple of days you can start locking it when your puppy is asleep and build up the time between him waking up and you opening it to let him out so that he doesn't expect to be let out immediately and panic or throw a tantrum when he's not. Bear in mind though, that certainly in the early days, he will need to go toilet fairly quickly after waking.

When you lure your puppy into the crate with a treat repeat what will be your command word as you do so... "in your crate", "crate" or "go in your crate" all work well; use a different word for his bed to save confusion and in the early days of crate training, the crate should be the only bed available to your puppy.

So, once he's allowed in the living room you'll have to decide whether you invest in another crate or take his night time one in with you... the crate in your living room won't be forever, you'll be able to replace it with a bed in a couple of months.

Up until the arrival of Ziggy in 2010, my puppies were trained to sleep downstairs from the first night; however, with Ziggy, I tried something different. After many discussions with my friend and colleague Ross McCarthy, I decided to bring Ziggy's crate into my bedroom and have him by the side of the bed for a couple of nights.

It worked ever so well that this is now how I start puppies off; that is if the new owners phone me prior to bringing the puppy home as once the puppy's slept downstairs I tend to leave them be.

So, if this is the first night of your puppy being home, when bedtime comes take your puppy's crate upstairs and put it by the side of your bed, close enough so that you can drape your hand on it if your puppy gets unsettled... try to keep everything calm and quiet and no 'cooing' over him at bedtime – take a matronly approach and you'll do fine.

When you hear your puppy start to stir (properly as opposed to just changing position), get straight up with no fuss and only the dimmest of lights and carry puppy down to the toileting area; as soon as he's done straight back to bed for both of you, giving him the tiniest of tiny treats as you pop him in his crate... you can now ignore him or just let your arm drape across the crate until it's time to get up.

After a couple of nights with your puppy beside you, start edging the crate out of the room and on to the landing; before you know it, your puppy will be sleeping quietly and confidently downstairs.

Even the professionals can get it wrong, especially with their own, and so a word of warning with the stuffed kongs; please don't make the mistake that I did with Ziggy and give them in the middle of the night to help your puppy settle back down - within a couple of days he was demanding his 4 a.m. kong!

Establishing a routine

It takes a bit of effort, and a bit of forethought, but establishing a routine for your little bundle of fun is worth it; not only for your puppy but for you too.

When you first bring your puppy home he'll be on four meals a day, so working, snoozing and training around them will make it much easier for you.

For the first couple of weeks try to set up a routine that goes something like toilet, train, play, feed and then in the crate for an hour or so to sleep off the learning, fun and food; then hanging around with you for an hour or so and then back in the crate for an hour with a toy and a stuffed kong.

Then it is train, play, feed and then in the crate for an hour or so to sleep off the learning, fun and food; then hanging around with you for an hour or so and then back in the crate for an hour with a snuggly toy and a kong. Then it's train, play, feed and then in the crate for an hour or so... you've got the gist of this haven't you?

If you can, have your puppy out of his crate with you for a couple of hours after his teatime / evening meal so that you can pop him away and have a much-needed puppy free half an hour (with your puppy in his crate in a different room) before bringing puppy in with you for an hour or so before bed.

It's a really good idea not to spend all your time with your puppy. Leaving him on his own will give him a chance to learn how to be comfortable in his skin, will help prevent separation anxiety further down the line and will give him a chance to assimilate all that he's learned in the last few hours – something he'll find difficult to do when his exciting new family are around.

It's important for you too... you need to get some down time without worrying about what your puppy is doing and if you should be doing this or that with him. If you find it stressful leaving him or if he whines, then check his needs have been met (toilet, food, water, cuddle) and go run yourself a hot bath; chances are when you come back downstairs he'll be sound asleep.

Remember to pick up the water a couple of hours before bed (giving him a sip or two if the weather's warm) to give your puppy a chance to 'empty the tanks' before bedtime and no exciting play an hour before bed!

Always train before feeding rather than feeding and then training; your puppy will be keener for the treats if he's hungry, and at this early stage you won't know what really motivates him other than an empty tummy, however if you find you have a bit of a 'piranha' for a puppy, or a puppy that gets completely over the top with food, you might find that training after feeding is kinder on your fingers... and your patience!

Remember however, there's no reason not to train your puppy without food and in 'the good old days' only trick trainers used food for dog training.

When I was growing up in the North East it was unheard of to buy training treats for your dog, actually thinking about it, I'm not sure they even existed; you just trained them by showing the dog what you wanted by physically putting your dog in that position and making a fuss of them when they got it right.

If you use the training treats correctly and phase them out as quickly as you can, then you should get good lasting results while making it easier to train your dog.

The Rottweiler.

Believed to be descended from the Roman drover dog, the Rottweiler is a strong, powerful dog that can be territorial and protective as well as a loving and faithful companion; but only to a leader that he respects.

Leadership in action

From the second you pick your puppy up you are his leader; initially this is a default position, however, by the time your puppy is between twelve and sixteen weeks the position has to be earned, therefore do yourself, your family and your puppy a favour and start as you mean to go on.

That doesn't mean booming at your puppy or getting cross, rather it means working out how you want your adult dog to behave and start moulding your puppy to fit that picture.

Leadership is about maintaining discipline and reinforcing those boundaries within our daily routines will instil them.

Leadership is about protecting our puppy and our dog from harm. It's about taking control of situations that we find ourselves in, so that our dogs can relax as they don't have to.

Leadership is about providing food, water, shelter, love and companionship and helping our puppy to develop into the best dog he can be.

In these early days of puppy ownership, you'll draw more upon the guiding and teaching elements of leadership; taking time out to train your puppy and to really make sure he understands what you're asking him to do, and taking time out to just be with him, having him lie at your feet or on his bed while you're watching TV or working.

Introducing your resident dog

If you already have a dog at home, it's a good idea to keep them separate for at least the first 24 hours; when you're with your puppy your adult dog can be out of the room, and when your puppy's resting in his crate you can make a fuss of your adult dog.

It's especially important, during this time, that your resident dog doesn't feel pushed sideways, as you don't want him to feel threatened by the puppy, however, you need to have at least a day of one on one bonding with your puppy.

Because your puppy and your dog speak the same language, your puppy will be more inclined to bond with your dog first; you need this time for your puppy to look at you as his family first, before he looks to bond with your dog, that way your puppy will be your puppy and not your dog's puppy.

When you're ready to introduce them, keep it low key. When your puppy has been toileted and is back in his (closed) crate, simply leave the door open to the room that he is in and allow your dog to wander into the room. Call your dog to you and give him a fuss then go out of the room and take him with you.

It should be a quiet but 'interested in each other' affair; they'll know pretty much everything about each other prior to this little meeting due to their amazing noses, however, to see each other for the first time will always generate interest and a little bit of excitement from your puppy, hence doing this after toileting.

Continue with this quiet, intermittent interaction for the next day or so, making sure you fuss your adult dog so that he knows he's still important in the family and then one time, when they're both relaxed open the crate door, but be on hand and ready to step in if the excitement levels rise; it's your job to protect not only your puppy from being hurt from your adult dog, but your adult dog from being pestered and bullied by your puppy. As soon as it starts getting too much (normally after 5 minutes initially), put your puppy away for a bit of quiet time.

Early training

Other than toilet training, crate training and establishing a routine, the only other things that I would train a puppy is to 'sit', what 'no' means, to 'hang out with me' (which quickly becomes lead walking and is described later in this chapter), and to accept being led around by the collar.

If you practice the 'hanging out with me' technique as many times during the day as you can, by the time you can take your puppy out you should, with a bit of luck, have pretty much mastered loose lead walking.

You can work your way through training your puppy the other exercises but, as puppies are little sponges, it would be easier to start sooner rather than later while your puppy is still hanging on your every word, so to speak... however if you find time is a bit tight, then the areas to concentrate on are 'Out and about with your dog', 'Instilling good behaviour at home' and 'What every puppy should know'.

Hold the collar and treat

If your breeder has put little coloured collars on the puppies while still in the litter to identify who's who, then this little exercise is going to be so much easier for you; if not, well you may get a tantrum or two... and that's okay, nothing to worry about; it's just your puppy adjusting to wearing a collar.

Do this little routine at least once a day and as you do so check the fit of the collar; puppies grow at an alarming rate and it's so easy for the collar to get very tight very quickly – you should be aiming for the collar to be loose enough to get two fingers side by side underneath it but tight enough so that it doesn't get caught on anything that your puppy squeezes under.

Initially simply say your puppy's name, smile at him and pop a finger under the collar; give him a stroke with the other hand and then give him a treat (while still holding the collar).

After you've done this a few times lure him into a sit with the treat by slowly lifting the treat over his head in an up and over movement (see training the sit for the full technique); yup, you've guessed it, while you're still holding the collar.

When puppy is happily accepting the two little routines, while holding his collar, encourage him to you and then start moving around ever so slightly so that your puppy gets used to being led around by his collar... you can now start phasing out the treats and toggle between sometimes giving him a stroke and smile, sometimes giving him a treat, and sometimes whipping a little toy out of your pocket and having a quiet play.

Realistically you can work through the above three steps in a day or two, providing you do it five or six times throughout the day. Puppies really are little sponges and are so desperate to gain the approval of their new family, so give them something to tire their brains out and that's taught in little steps, so that he's getting it right and receiving the praise and approval he needs, which in turn, will motivate him to get it right next time.

Sit

Teaching your puppy to sit is one of the most important things you'll ever do. Once it's taught, if you don't want your puppy to do something you just say sit and his bottom goes down interrupting any behaviour that you want to stop.

You can train this little exercise quite informally by just scooping your puppy's hind end towards you with one hand while the other steadies him at the front end and popping him in a sit. In the early days he'll be almost sitting on your hand; say very quietly "sit" as you do so and stroke him in that position.

To more formally train him to sit, take a piece of treat and take it to his nose; this is to get his nose working for you and to get him really interested in what you're doing, then take it above his head and, in an up and over movement, slowly taking the food towards his hindquarters. As he puts his backside down on the ground say "sit", tell him what a good boy he is and give him the treat.

If you find he starts walking backwards then slow down your movement; whereas if he tries to jump up lower your hand as you've raised it up too high too soon. Remember it's the action of sitting that gets the treat so no giving him the sweetie (dog treat) until his bum is down!

Once you've got your co-ordination sorted out you may want to start holding the treat between your index finger and thumb in a 'pincer' grip with the rest of your fingers straight.

This will help prepare your puppy for the sit/stop/stay hand signal which you'll use later - when you stop training with food in a month or so, all you'll need to do is straighten out your index finger and you have a conditioned hand signal, similar to that used by a policeman to stop traffic, or, in our case, our dog.

Once your puppy knows how to sit nicely in front of you it's time to start teaching him to sit at your side as well.

While your puppy's sitting, use a little treat to keep him still (only let him sniff it at the minute) then turn yourself away from your puppy so that he is sitting by your left leg (or right leg if you want him to walk on that side).

Take a tiny to baby step forward, encouraging your puppy to come with you by luring him with the food and after he's moved a pace or two, slide the treat up your leg; his nose will follow and say "sit". He's already been taught that sit means 'put bottom on the ground' and so his backside will go down.

Hanging out "with me"

Rather than call this 'heelwork' or 'walking to heel' or even 'walking on a loose lead' I thought I'd call it hanging out with me, as that's pretty much all that we want our puppy to do at the minute.

When your puppy is with you, slowly turn away from him, patting your left leg as you do so and to encourage him to come with you, praise with a "good boy" and after a few paces bend down and give him a stroke, a smile, and, if you feel so inclined, a treat.

You can also start to lure him around to your leg with a treat by slowly drawing him from the front in a little anti-clockwise circle around to your left leg (or clockwise to your right leg) and saying, "with me" as you do so, walking a couple of paces with puppy by your leg and then giving him the treat and a stroke.

If your puppy's behind you or off to the side then lure him to your leg on the move so that he comes up alongside you... when he's by your leg say "with me", walk a couple of paces with him by your side and then give him the treat and a stroke.

It really doesn't matter which side you walk your puppy on as long as you are consistent and don't let him weave back and forwards in front or behind you; not only will it be a nightmare to train loose lead walking, but you'll end up tripping over him or standing on his little paws.

If you decide a bit later on that you want to do some sort of activity with your dog, for example agility or competitive obedience, then you'll be able to train the position according to the discipline that you decide to get involved with; this, for now, is simply putting in the foundations to make your dog walks of the future less stressful and more enjoyable.

NO!

Until you've conditioned the word, 'no' has absolutely no meaning whatsoever to your puppy.

As a child we learn what 'no' means from our parents as they use it along with a negative consequence, either removing us from something or something from us, then as we get older they may reason us out of doing something but generally it's a case of "no, don't do that" or "no, don't do that because..."

Unfortunately, your puppy has absolutely no concept of reasoning and neither will your adult dog. The part of the brain that deals with reasoning and starts to develop in us when we're about three years old doesn't, and never will, exist in the canine brain. This is why we have to be absolutely consistent with what we tell our dogs to do and why we have to be very black and white with no shades of grey.

To condition your puppy to the word 'no', quite simply the first time he does something that you don't want him to do, make a bit of a drama about it; slap the bench or drop a heavy book and say "NO!" very loudly.

Your puppy will more than likely look at you, and you will be watching with a look of outrage and disgust on your face... turn on your heel and walk to the other side of the room. By displaying outrage and turning away you're communicating to your puppy that you're *really* not happy and, at this young age, your puppy will feel excluded from his pack which he won't want to feel again.

Give it a second or two and call your puppy over, scoop him into a sit (if he doesn't look as if he's going to do it on his own) and calmly give him a stroke... misdemeanour forgotten.

Fiddle and Faff

Some puppies love to be stroked and fiddled about with and some puppies don't, however, *all* puppies need to be taught to enjoy attention and to relax when being attended to.

Try to spend at least five minutes a day, especially in the early days while your puppy will still comfortably fit on your knee, sitting on the floor with him either on your lap, between your legs or beside you... after the mad-half-hour is normally the best time to do it (which is generally mid-evening) or when your puppy is feeling snoozy after he's eaten and toileted.

Smooth your hands all over your puppy's little body, remembering to include the tail and the paws as well as the ears. Put words on them as you do so; it will pay dividends when you visit the vets as you'll be able to say to puppy "ears" as your vet looks in his ears and it won't be strange or scary for him.

Remember to also cuddle him in your arms and plant kisses on him, once he's stopped trying to eat your hair, lips, nose and cheeks.

Although hugging is not part of the dog's communication system, it is very much a part of ours, and the more we can teach a dog to tolerate what comes naturally to humans, the 'safer' our dogs will be, although it's got to be said, no dog is 100% bombproof, we can at least, stack the odds in our dog's favour through familiarity.

This fiddle and faff session is also the perfect time to teach your puppy some self-control when we sit on the floor with them by folding them into a sit or collapsing them into a down.

To fold your puppy into a sit, put a hand on their chest and 'scoop' their bottom under them so that they're pretty much sitting on your hand, and slowly and quietly remove it so that they're sitting on the floor... saying "sit" as you do so.

To collapse your puppy into a down from a sitting position, put a hand on a shoulder and gently rock them sideways until they relax and lie down or, if they're tiny, lift them off their feet and put them down gently on their side... remembering to say "down" and gently stroke them as you do so.

Instilling good behaviour at home

We all dream and romanticise about what our adult dog will be like, but unfortunately, for the most part, our daydreams skip from beautiful, cute, adorable puppy to well-trained dog with a fabulous personality that we can take anywhere, and kind of fuzzes out the hard work and heartache in the middle.

If we can have a really good idea of what we're aiming for, apply a bit of discipline in our everyday life (for us as well as our puppy) and keep in our mind that we're not 'training' (which tends to be slotted into the 'later' category) then we're definitely going to be on the winning side.

Remember that as far as our puppy is concerned, all he needs to know is what is acceptable to his pack, what's not acceptable to his pack and what he can get away with; everything else is just 'tricks'.

Sit for Attention

For me, this is the cornerstone of your training. If you can establish early on that your puppy will only ever get attention when he's sitting, I can pretty much guarantee that he will come over and sit in front of you when he wants a stroke. This means that jumping up for attention or pawing at you and chewing on you won't be part of his repertoire; he will simply sit.

Sit will become your puppy's default position.

If you can be strong and insist that everyone who comes in to contact with your puppy ensures he sits for attention too, then you have just made going out with your puppy so much easier and are half way to having a dog that is trained for life.

Four on Floor

The only time your puppy shouldn't have four paws on the floor, is when he's in your arms.

Allowing your puppy to jump up at you may seem like a good idea, and cute and adorable but trust me... it won't be so cute when he's an adult dog covered in fox poo or rancid badger and you're in your best clobber... or when friends come to visit and are bare, or stocking legged and your dog rakes his claws down them.

Allowing your puppy to jump up or bounce up and down on his hind legs can have a massive negative impact on the state of his joint health.

The Chihuahua.

Although small, there's absolutely nothing tiny about his personality...
a characterful feisty little dog who is a great companion with a
surprising amount of stamina.

Research is currently underway (winter 2017) to see how much influence genetics has on hip and elbow dysplasia in the face of bangs, knocks and over-use. See the Optimum Health section for more information on the PUPscan project.

Resisting the urge to have your puppy up on the settee with you is much easier when you know that every time they clamber up they are putting a massive and unnecessary strain on their cruciate ligament and hips, and that every time they jump off the settee their wrists, elbows and shoulders are jarred through the impact of all of their weight travelling through them at speed.

Start as you mean to go on and insist your puppy has four on the floor.

On your bed

Teaching your puppy to go on his bed isn't that different to teaching him to go into his crate; the only difference (apart from the word) is that teaching him to go in his crate means you'll shut the door to restrain him whereas with the bed you'll lure him into a down with a treat and use your presence to keep him there.

Initially that will mean giving him another treat while on his bed, but then, once he knows he's supposed to lie there until you release him, you can instead, use your body to prevent him getting off by simply standing in front him... by 'body blocking' him.

When you first start teaching this command, have his bed at your feet and then over time edge it to the area you want it to end up in; this will make the training much easier and by the time you get any kind of distance between you and your puppy, he will be happy to settle away from you.

Feeding Time

Once you've trained a sit and your puppy knows that to get the treat his bottom needs to go on the floor, exploit the association between 'sit' and 'food' before you put his dinner down for him.

The key at feeding time, is not to tell him to sit, rather for him to figure it out for himself that he doesn't get fed unless he's sitting.

Hold the food bowl in front of you so that he has to look up; when he sits put the bowl down for him... if he goes to get up just lift it up again but not so high so that as soon as he sits you can put it down.

Before you know it, you'll have the food bowl down and your puppy sitting. To start off with, as soon as the food is down, give your puppy his release command so that he knows it's okay to eat, however try to build it up so that you can put food down and then pause before you release him.

Occasionally add food to your puppy's bowl while he's eating so that he associates you approaching his bowl as a good thing.

Removing his bowl whilst he's eating doesn't mean you'll be able to remove it when he's an adult; it will just make him wolf his food down when see's you approaching, or worse, become protective and guarding of his food.

For this reason, I never recommend taking the bowl away from your dog until he has completely finished eating. Think how you would feel if you were half way through your dinner and someone took away your plate or whisked it away before you'd had a chance to mop up the gravy with a bit of bread...

Eating is such an enjoyable thing for a dog; and is what allows him to survive – let him nose his bowl around and give it a really good lick before you consider taking it away.

Doorway Manners

Doors and doorways hold so much interest for puppies (and for grown up dogs too for that matter) as there's always something happening on the other side... the saying 'the grass is always greener on the other side of the fence' springs to mind here.

At this young age it's all about exploring and the excitement of getting out of the door and to somewhere new. As your little puppy grows, however, there will also be an element of competition over who gets out of the door first, as the first out will get to the toy on the other side or get to go play in the garden first.

It is in this area of the doorway that puppies really can learn to barge and more importantly from their perspective, that they can barge into you and you just step back and let them go first: not the best demonstration of leadership I'm sure you'll agree.

After you

While your puppy is still very young, position yourself between your puppy and the door, and, use the outside of your leg, sorry, 'silently' use the outside of your leg, to gently guide them away from the door as you slowly open it. If your puppy goes to move forward use your leg to gently push him back again.

When you can open it without your puppy moving forward, *and it's safe to do so*, then you can either let your puppy go through first or can go through calling your puppy with you as you go.

When your puppy is bit older, around twelve weeks, you can start closing the door in front of your puppy, however, if you've been doing the above since he was nine or ten weeks then you probably won't need to do this.

Quite simply as you go to open the door, instead of opening it fully just open it an inch or so and then close it with a resounding snap, again you'll do this without saying anything. Repeat a couple of times until your puppy is backing off... you're aiming as you move into the next chapter of the book to be able to stand with a door open and your puppy not wanting to go through it without permission.

Please be careful with the old wooden style doors that have 'lips' on them and don't practice this technique on them at all as puppies are incredibly quick and you can catch a little paw between the threshold and the lip causing damage... practice the routine on other doors.

Remember to use this little routine of opening a tiny bit and then shutting the door with a snap to teach your puppy not to barge out of his crate when you open the door; good manners, even at a very early age, are absolutely essential. I have found that it's easier to start with doors opening away from you.

And, although it should go without saying, I'm going to say it anyway; practice doorway manners after you've got a good idea of your puppy's toilet routine and once your puppy can hold his bladder a little otherwise you'll either cause a toilet accident or make the 'urge' go away and cause an accident later.

Bringing people in to your home

In the early days, whether you're going to the door for the postman or to bring people in, leave your puppy in his crate or, if he's not in it when the door goes, then put him in it.

If you're worried about taking too long to answer the door then put a little notice up to say that you're puppy training so may take a little longer than usual; bear in mind many postmen and delivery men get bit, or live in fear of being bit, and so will be absolutely cool with waiting an extra minute or two and will probably appreciate you making the effort to train your puppy.

Once your puppy is happy on the lead, so hopefully around the 12-14-week mark, then you'll take him with you to the door. Invest in two or three spare leads and have one hanging on the back of the door where your crate is, one on the back of the kitchen door and another by the front door.

When the door goes encourage your puppy to come with you to the nearest lead, pop him in a sit and put his lead on, then, using a treat, have him walk to heel to the door and sit when you get there. Open the door, beam a smile at the person waiting and say that you're puppy training; remember every time your puppy goes to get up put him in a sit.

When you've finished dealing with the person at the door and the door is closed, give your puppy a treat, release him and take his lead off.

If you find you're struggling with manners at the front door and are feeling pressured by making the deliveryman wait, you can always have a bowl of wrapped sweets to offer them while you're working at puppy training; it will give them something to do and take a bit of pressure off you as you desperately try to keep your puppy's backside on the ground.

A word of warning when dealing with people at the door; do not let them stroke your puppy or give him a treat... once he's trained then it's your choice, but initially I would advise against it, as your puppy might think the doorbell is the signal for a yummy treat and a bit of fuss and get thoroughly over-excited at the sound of it.

Come in...

When you answer the door to invite people into your home, go through the same routine as you would for the postman. Once your puppy is sitting nicely by your side, invite your guests in (reminding them to ignore the puppy for the time being) and using a treat, walk your puppy to heel into whichever room you and your guests are going to be in.

Keeping your puppy on lead, either sit yourself down and stand on the lead or prop yourself up against a kitchen bench and stand on the lead... it's now everyone's job to ignore the puppy until he relaxes, when he does so you can very quietly take your foot off the lead. If he gets over excited or tries to jump all over your guests just take the lead again and pop him into a sit, give him a reward and stand on the lead again.

Remind your guests that they can stroke your puppy as much as they like providing he's sitting and his front feet are down.

If you have people come to visit before your puppy is happy being on a lead, very quietly let him out of his crate, toilet if need be and then ignore him until he relaxes – if he's jumping up at your guests then show them how to scoop him into a sitting position and quietly stroke him, thereby reinforcing your 'sit for attention' routine.

The more you teach him good manners around your family and friends the greater joy (and less stress) you will receive in return.

Not You!

This little command came about by accident when I lived in a house with amazing wooden floors that I didn't want scratched by my big dogs' claws. Every time I entered the room I dropped my hand down, palm facing them, pushed gently against their face and said, "not you".

In no time at all the dogs learned not to cross the threshold from the carpet in the family room to the wooden floor in the living room; it wasn't a "let's create a new exercise" moment, rather a getting on with family life one.

And it's an exercise that is loved by everyone who has come across it as the dogs really understand the meaning very quickly due to the principles applied; we really are talking dog in its basic form as we're training with body language, space management and touch, which is how they communicate with each other. I use it with my puppies to teach them not to follow me upstairs or into rooms that they're not allowed in.

And 'not you' means just that... I don't want you to come with me, but you don't have to hold your position as you would with a stay – you're free to move around providing you don't follow me.

As humans we like to say something to our puppy as we leave the room (remembering that in the early days that we would only leave puppy in the room if there was another person there to look after him otherwise we would put him in his crate) so 'not you' would fit the bill perfectly.

So, as you go to walk out of the room, say "not you", put your hand in front of your puppy's face so that you're blocking him from moving forward and then move off without him; in time you can just use the hand down towards his face to indicate he's not coming out of the room with you or just drop the communication entirely.

It's much easier to train the 'not you' exercise when you move between rooms with different floor surfaces, for example lino to carpet or at a narrow space; doorways and arches work great.

Go to walk into a room with your puppy loosely beside you and as you cross the threshold reach down with your open hand in front of your puppy's face, say "not you" and push *towards* your puppy; if he continues walking, gently push his face backwards, say "not you!" and keep walking, go a stride or two and then go back to your puppy, praise him and forget all about going into the room without him, instead head back the way you came.

Build it up so that you can go into the other room, have a walk around and come back out without your puppy following you.

Playtime

Playing games is such an intrinsic part of your puppy's psychological makeup and while in the litter will spend a lot of his time playing with his siblings. As you now know, this 'play' is about the puppy learning the skills that will ensure he stays alive and at the rank that he feels he ought to be at.

Playing on their own with toys is about taking some of their energy away, learning how to wrestle things to the ground as well as stalking and pouncing; toys help with teething and they're fun boredom breakers.

When dogs play as adults they will always 'pull their punches', so to speak, and although play includes an element of contest it doesn't include competition as dogs will quite often put themselves in vulnerable positions for a good game of rough and tumble with each other.

In the way that dogs have 'rules' with each other when playing, it's important for us to have them too as the last thing we want is for him to play the stalking, pouncing, attacking game with us, more so when there are children in the house.

Playing with puppy should be kept calm, no rough housing or encouraging the puppy to bite or scrabble at us and no playing pull with a toy, until the adult teeth are in, as you run the risk of pinging out baby teeth or misaligning his jaw if you pull hard to the side.

If your puppy keeps trying to incite you into a game of pull or tug, then put the toy on the ground and hold it there with your hand so that your puppy can pull without you pulling back as that is when the damage is done.

Without getting overly technical about it, a dog's jaw, unlike ours, never fuses at the chin to make it one solid bone, rather the two sides knit together on a bit of cartilage called the mandibular symphysis, a bit like how our pelvis goes together at the front.

Just like the front of the pelvis (the pubic symphysis) opening when women give birth, so too can trauma cause the manibular symphysis to move out of alignment; this does get a bit more robust as the dog matures (although a mandibular symphyseal fracture is not uncommon in adult dogs), but as a puppy it is less so and is something that I'm always quite precious about.

Games of chase, even with a little puppy, should be banned from day one... you and I both know that at some point you're not going to be able to catch him, either that's because he's faster than you or can get under the table where you can't get to him.

At that point you have quite successfully communicated to your puppy that he can't be caught if he doesn't want to be, which really doesn't bode well for your recall training.

What every puppy should know

It wasn't that many years ago when the backbone of every dog training class consisted, first and foremost, of how to train an obedient dog.

More and more though, I've seen the basics of responsible dog ownership and the common-sense foundations being brushed aside for trick training. That's not to say that trick training isn't great fun and a lovely thing to do with your dog, because it is; but it really needs to come *after* the basics rather than *instead of*.

I've seen lots of behaviour cases where the dogs can shake paws, high five and play dead, but won't come when called, jump up and counter surf. If only the owners put as much time and effort into training the foundations as the tricks, their homes, and their dogs, would be a lot less stressful.

Do yourself and your puppy a favour and spend a little time each day training the basics. It doesn't need to be a long hard slog; just a couple of minutes when you're waiting for the kettle to boil or during the ad break of your favourite TV programme.

The exercises that follow, are, for me, the most important things to teach your puppy; training them will keep him safe and make it a joy to share your life with him.

Work your way through them, focussing on a couple of exercises a day and before you know it your puppy will not only be an adolescent, but he'll be a well-trained adolescent too.

Come when called

When our puppies are very young we are the most important thing in their lives, however, as they start to get a little bit more confident and start to explore, we can, quite quickly and without realising it's happening, fade into the background. Not only do we become unimportant (apart from at mealtimes) but, as real life takes over, for us and our puppy, we become uninteresting.

It happens so slowly and incrementally that we simply aren't aware of it until it's an issue; we might have to call of our puppy a couple of times before we get a response or, when we've trained our pup to go on his bed, he starts to meander off to the side to collect a toy on the way or have a sniff.

These are little signs that we need to be more insistent in our training...

insist our puppy finishes an exercise that we are teaching rather than reward him for 'kind of' doing it.

It is this, 'not quite' doing as they're told, or having to repeat an instruction (once trained) a number of times, that will play havoc when training a recall. Just think about it for a second; if you were told to do something 3, 4 or even 5 times before the person telling you 'meant' business, would you stop doing that really fun thing the first time you were told to? Or would you push your luck?

Yeah, me too... unfortunately we can't do this with our puppies as it will have such a negative impact on our recall and the recall is something that a dog needs to do first time every time, as not only is it a potential life-saver and keeping you on the right side of the law, but it's a fabulous thing to have and makes your walks at worst stress-free and at best, great fun.

Need more convincing?

Go onto Google, or Youtube, and type in "Fenton deer chase" and you will see the most cringe-worthy footage of a black Labrador causing havoc chasing deer in Richmond Park. Sorry, chasing deer is an understatement... this dog caused a stampede of a large herd of deer across roads and all you hear is the owner cussing and swearing while running after his dog.

If you ever think, 'I will train my puppy tomorrow', think FENTON!

The Recall Game

When we first start training a recall, we keep it really informal and fun; we want our dogs and puppies to want to come back to us; we say "come" they say, "how fast?".

We can play the recall game from the second we bring our puppy home, and I'm sure by the time you get this far in the book you've been doing it already.

The first part is really just to make yourself interesting to your puppy, so that your puppy wants to be with you. Emptying the washing machine? 'my favourite thing in the whole wide world'. Tidying up? 'my favourite thing in the whole wide world'. Going in the kitchen? 'my favourite thing in the whole wide world' Yup, that's what it will be like (or should be like) when our puppy is very young... so exploit it.

When you're together and your puppy is looking in your general direction, make a silly noise and pat your legs; as your puppy starts coming towards you give him a big beaming smile and say his name followed by "come". When he's with you give him a sweetie, a cuddle or have a little play with him.

When he's a little bit older (10-11 weeks) and there's more than one of you at home, you can play a little 'ping-pong' with him. Set it up so that everyone has a couple of treats in their pockets and are standing in different parts of the room. The person furthest away from puppy will make a silly noise and when puppy looks, bend down and pat their legs and say 'puppy's name' "come", and hold the treat down by their knees. When the puppy comes, lure the puppy into a sit and then, taking the collar with one hand, give the puppy the treat with the other.

Releasing the collar and 'ruffling' or gently patting the puppy's head (to dismiss or release the puppy), the next person will make a silly noise and when puppy looks, bend down and pat their legs and say 'puppy's name' "come", and hold the treat down by their knees. When the puppy comes, lure the puppy into a sit and then, taking the collar with one hand, give the puppy the treat with the other.

Releasing the collar and 'ruffling' or gently patting the puppy's head (to dismiss or release the puppy), the next person will... you get the idea don't you.

If you find your puppy is turning away from you too soon or 'dismissing' you, do a gentle little finger drum roll, as you would on a desk, on your puppy's back end as he turns away with a "what are you doing?" in a disapproving tone of voice, remembering to smile and praise when he returns.

Silently luring your puppy into a sit when he comes and then holding his collar before rewarding him with a treat or a stroke, is establishing the routine ready for popping his lead on after recalling him on a walk. By repeating it over and over now around the home, you're creating a learned behaviour that will be massively beneficial in the future.

Start your recall training in the most boring of places and really set yourself up to succeed quickly with this exercise; pick up all of the toys and 'distractions', don't train a tired 'fractious' puppy or when people are coming home or leaving as that will make it harder for you.

When you've cracked the recall in one room introduce it in another one and then in the garden, however, you shouldn't be looking to let your puppy off in a public place until you've got 100% recall everywhere else and you've trained the rest of the exercises in this section... if you've really 'nailed' it then probably around the 6 months mark.

Down

Training the down is such a valuable exercise to teach your puppy as it forms the basis of teaching him to settle down while you're relaxing and to go on his bed.

Having a puppy, and then a dog, that can't switch off and settle down is so stressful, not just for you but for your puppy too; and if you have wooden or laminate flooring it will drive you mad... all that click click click of their claws pacing back and forwards or, as Spud used to when we first got him, round and round the rug.

Pacing dogs can fatigue their adrenal system because the dog is constantly on the go, thereby burning energy and potentially losing condition and lean muscle, plus, they never mentally switch off which means their body can't rest and rejuvenate.

In the same way that parents of young children insist on mid- morning and afternoon naps, so too do we need to teach our puppies to lie down on command and 'be still'.

Put a couple of tiny treats in your hand and let your puppy know that you have them. Lure him into the down by slowly placing your hand between / in front of your puppy's front legs. Keep your hand on the floor and give your puppy a second or two to figure out what he's meant to do.

If he bows and stays in the bow position, fold him into a down with the other hand by gently pushing on his raised backend - push away from you rather than straight down so you're not putting pressure on his pelvis. If he doesn't lie down and doesn't bow, then put the heel of your hand on his shoulder blades with your fingertips towards his backend and fold him down.

When he's in the down position, release the treats as you remove your hand and say "down". Always reward your puppy for downing by putting the treats on the floor rather than from your hand as this will (hopefully) keep him in the down position as you remove your hand rather than popping out of the position as soon as you move.

Once your puppy gets the gist of what down means, you can start to stand upright while your puppy is still in the down position by popping another couple of treats between his front paws as you stand up – remember to say "down" as you do so to encourage him to stay in that position.

Stand

Teaching the stand is another one of the fundamentals of puppy training; in the months and years to come you will be so glad you invested some time in training this little exercise.

Why? Well it's great for when you're grooming, drying off after a wet walk or much later, doing a stay in filthy weather whilst you're clambering through a fence, however, for me the most important reason for training the stand is for your visits to the vet.

Your vet cannot get the thermometer where it needs to go if your dog is sitting, and it's pretty awkward when the dog is in a down – for this to happen easily and without stress for all concerned your dog should be standing. Standing, not shuffling forward as the last thing you want is for your puppy to shuffle off the table or, later, be part of a comedy skit where he's walking in a circle around you whilst your vet is following along behind trying to hang on to a thermometer.

Before you train the stand though you first need to train either the sit or the down as your puppy must be in one of these positions to start with.

Pop your puppy in either a sit or a down and give him a little treat or simply praise him; turn to face your puppy and very slowly lure him forward with a treat until he stands.

Once he's standing let him nibble on the treat and say "stand", "good boy, stand"; if he sits or lies down, just lure him forward again.

When your puppy is happily standing still and nibbling on the treat in your hand it's time to start fiddling with him, bearing in mind this exercise is for grooming, drying and for the vet to do their 'bits'.

Slowly, calmly and gently start to stroke your puppy with your free hand; if he tries to move away keep your hand still rather than removing it as all that will teach him is that if he moves away from your hand you'll stop. Stroke the full length of his back and introduce stroking his ears, stroking his legs, lifting his paws, stroking his tail and putting your flat hand between his hind legs.

It may take a wee while to get to the point where you're able to have your puppy standing while you 'fiddle about' so don't rush it... slowly does it.

Leave it!

This has got to be one the favourite exercises that I teach, not only for new puppy owners, but new dog trainers love it too, and many have incorporated it into their classes. It is easy to teach, the puppies (and dogs) pick it up incredibly quickly and it is such a valuable thing to train.

However, train this exercise at a different time to everything else, preferably at the end of a session, as you'll be teaching your puppy to turn away from food

Hold a small to tiny treat in a pinch grip between your thumb and middle finger keeping your index finger tucked in. Offer your puppy the treat and gently say "Good, take it". Do this at least four or five times.

Then offer your puppy the treat and do not say anything. When he goes to take the treat, lift up your index finger and gently tap the side of his nose with it saying "leave it" as you do so.

As soon as your puppy turns away from the treat, regardless of how slight (and a pause or hesitation counts), then give it to him with a "good, take it". Do this another couple of times and call it a day for this session.

By saying "good" followed by "take it" you're giving your puppy permission to take the treat from your hand. If you make a habit of saying this whenever you hand feed your puppy (training the sit, down etc., excepted), in a very short space of time your puppy won't take food from someone's hand without permission to do so.

In what feels like no time at all you'll have a hand signal of a raised index finger coupled with saying 'leave it' to turn your puppy's nose away from things; give it a little bit longer and you'll be able to use either command or hand signal with great effect.

Loose lead walking
Getting the lead on

At some point you're going to have to introduce your puppy to the lead. Most puppies will try to chew it or bite at it - if this is the case for your puppy, cover the lead with bitter apple spray (see chewing things below) and try again.

If he's insistent then train the 'leave it!' command for a couple of days and then try again applying the 'leave it!' if necessary, however, if you wait until your puppy is hanging out with you, sitting and is used to you leading him a few paces by his collar before introducing the lead, then hopefully you won't have a problem.

Pop your puppy in a sit in front of you and reward (at this early stage it can be a food treat but in time a 'good boy' with a smile will suffice), attach the lead while he's sitting, tell him what a good boy he is and give him another little sweetie.

Leaving your puppy sitting, pop yourself into the heel position and lure him forward a pace or two saying "with me" as you do so... after a couple of paces pop him in a sit, take the lead off and have a play with him or give him a treat.

Do this a couple of times going no more than a couple of paces before taking off the lead; give it a couple of days before embarking on training loose lead walking.

Walking to heel

Before I put the lead on my puppies I like them to think that the best place in the world is by my left leg, which makes putting the lead on much easier as I have less to think about and the puppy isn't distracted by a bit of nylon dangling from my hands.

Take a treat in your left hand and position yourself so that your puppy is on your left; it doesn't matter what position your puppy is in to start off with. Put the treat up to your puppy's nose and walk a couple of 'baby' paces luring your puppy with you and then feed him; remember to keep your hand near or slightly behind your 'jean seam' as it will help prevent your puppy from dashing in front of you. You will have to bend down so remember to take lots of breaks not only for your puppy's sake but for your back's sake too.

Now is the time to introduce the word heel (or whatever word you're planning on using to mean walk beside me) and as you're walking with your puppy by your leg, just say "heel, good boy... heel". Remember to take it slowly though as he's still very much a baby.

Repeat the above until you and your puppy can comfortably do about 10 baby paces interspersed with sweeties, then start withholding the treat for a couple of paces; turn the *back* of your hand toward your puppy so that your hand stays in the same position, but your puppy cannot get the food as it's facing to the front, then turn your fingers towards your puppy and reward.

Over the next couple of days, you can start to play with this little routine by turning your hand away and back a couple of times without actually feeding your puppy.

Build up so that you're doing about ten paces without feeding your puppy then feed your puppy, lure him into a sit, reward him and end the session.

Once you can do about ten paces without feeding you can also start to stand up. Rather than turning your hand away stand up instead, then, to keep your puppy interested and keen, bend down and give him a sniff of the treat before you stand up again.

Remember the bigger the puppy the less you have to bend – you may even get away with leaning sideways or doing a bit of a side bend which is better for both you and your puppy as your face will be further away from his, thereby not encouraging him to jump up.

If he does try to jump up it's likely to be because you have your treat too high for him to reach comfortably but low enough for him to think he can snatch it out of your hand by jumping at you – either bring the treat down to his nose or move it higher up out of temptations way.

If he gets ahead of you turn slowly away from him and walk the other way, patting your left leg and saying his name to get his attention along with the 'with me' command that you were using initially; once he's walked to heel for a couple of strides give him a treat.

Come to heel

In the same way you taught your puppy to move to the heel position while working through the "with me" exercise, so too can you teach your puppy to move to the "heel" position from the front. It's taught the same but with a different command and ends with your puppy a bit closer to your leg.

Regardless of what position your puppy is in front of you, use a treat to lure him around to your leg by slowly drawing him from the front in a little anti-clockwise circle around to your left leg (or clockwise to your right leg) and saying, "heel" as you do so. You can then either walk a couple of paces with puppy by your leg or lure him into a sit by your left leg before giving him the treat and a stroke.

Stay
Introducing the Stay

Teaching a stay is a gradual process of pausing... and then resuming.

If when you first started training your puppy to stay you bellowed 'stay' and strode off across the room, I would guarantee one of several things would happen; your puppy would cower, your puppy would follow you, your puppy would lie down and lick or scratch, your puppy would wander off. Why? Because unless you train your puppy to do something, he will do what makes him feel good.

Start your stay training with the sit exercise as this is generally the easiest one to work with as it's the first exercise we train, however, don't start until your puppy is confident sitting beside your leg as well as out in front... at that point, which will only be a few days if you train little and often, you can start morphing it into a stay.

When we teach our puppy to stay or stop, or when using the "not you" command, we tend to use a variation of the policeman's 'stop' hand signal; not only is it a clear hand signal but it's also a strong hand signal, blocking any forward movement.

Dogs, being masters of body language and the subtleties of weight distribution, respond really well to this blocking position and so we incorporate it into our training whenever we are leaving our dogs behind. So...

With your puppy sitting by your left leg, tell him 'stay' and drop your open palm towards your puppy and say 'stay'. Pause with your puppy in a sit, and then calmly praise and release him... and then do it again.

When you can pause and use the 'stay' word without your puppy squirming or moving, then say "stay", lean slightly away from your puppy so that you're putting a little bit of distance between your faces; say "stay" again and then stand up normally, reward and release.

Aim for your puppy to be able to 'stay' in one position for about five seconds before you start to move your feet.

Extending the Stay

It's more beneficial to increase the amount of time that your puppy is in a stay rather than the distance that you can get away from them without moving, although it's got to be said, when training in the local park the latter does look so much more impressive, however, plenty of time for that!

To start off we'll be looking at extending the amount of time your puppy can hold a position, which will reap the rewards when your puppy is older and going to the pub with you as you'll be able to pop him in a down stay under the table and enjoy your lunch or a pint.

Set up your puppy for the stay and this time, as you lean away with your shoulders, take your right leg out to the side and put your weight over it so you're really putting a bit of distance physically, and energetically, between you and your puppy while leaving your left foot beside them as a bit of a 'comfort blanket'.

Do this a few times and call it a day, for now. Next time you work on this little exercise, rather than returning to your puppy's side, repeat the hand signal and say "stay" and bring your left foot to join your right so that you're standing a pace away from your puppy. Take a breath and then return to your puppy's side.

Slowly build up moving sideways in the above fashion until you're a couple of paces away. When you can do this without your puppy following you, it's time to step away to the front.

Tell your puppy to 'stay' (verbal and hand signal together) and take a step to the front, turn to face your puppy, give him a huge smile and then return to his side; quietly praise and then release him.

When you can stand a pace in front of your puppy for 10 seconds then it's time to start adding a bit of distance and challenge. Instead of stopping and facing your puppy after one step, stop after two and then return to your puppy after 5 seconds.

After doing this a couple of times increase the count to 10 and then 15... then instead of returning to your puppy take a step back so you've now put 3 paces between you....

You can continue to build up like this until you're doing a minute or so, however, if you're going to be going for a long stay I would recommend you do it in a down and wait until puppy's a bit older.

If you need a target to work towards, aim for a 30 second sit-stay and a one minute down-stay when your dog is 6 months old.

The Steadiness Clock

You can, as your puppy gets steadier, start to walk around him to add a bit of challenge to your training. Once you've got to standing 2 paces away for 15 seconds, instead of returning to your dog, start walking out to the side and then back to the front, so if your dog was sitting in the centre of a clock face facing 12 o'clock, you would initially walk from 12 to 2, back to 12 and then return to your puppy.

Extend the steadiness clock slowly and surely until you can go all the way around the clock before returning to your puppy. The trick is to have your puppy sitting (or lying) confidently as you walk round to 5 and then all the way back through 12 to 7 and then back again without getting up; when he can do that you can continue all the way round.

This is a difficult little exercise and again, like the duration training, I would expect it to take around two to three months of training doing a little every other day while you're in the kitchen waiting for the kettle to boil. If your kitchen is laminate or lino, pop a little mat down for your puppy to sit on, so he doesn't slip and slide.

Target training the Stay

It sounds a little fancy doesn't it... target training the stay?

Well if you've popped your puppy on the mat as above, that's kind of what you're doing without realising it. By consistently using an item to place your puppy on as part of his stay training, he will start to look for the item to settle on.

Once he's got the gist of sitting and staying, or downing and staying, on the mat you can give it a name or a verbal cue "on your mat, good boy, stay!" or similar.

One of my friends trained his young Rottweiler to target stay on a roll up bamboo placemat, then when he went to the pub with his mates for lunch, he would put his dog in a down-stay on the mat.

Stop

It really doesn't matter whether you train your puppy to stop in the sit position or the down position, it only matters that you take time to train it.

Before you start training this though, make sure your puppy has a snappy sit beside you and is confident in the down, otherwise you'll get frustrated with him and he'll mess you around or lose his confidence in you.

Realistically you're looking to be training this between four and five months (so moving out of puppyhood and into adolescence) but definitely before you take the lead off away from home.

If your puppy's food motivated then start training 'stop' with a treat; if he's really toy motivated then use a toy, however once you start making a game of the training, toggle between the two so that your puppy never knows what reward will be forthcoming from your hand.

Have a tennis ball, small toy or a biscuit (Winalot Shapes are ideal) in your hand and 'tease' your puppy with it, encouraging him to follow your hand or chase the toy, without actually getting it.

Pretend to throw it just in front of you so that your puppy moves slightly away from you, as he turns towards you, raise the hand that has the toy in it and say 'sit' or 'down' - the second your puppy complies throw the treat or the toy directly towards his mouth.

You need to keep your arm up in the air and throw from that position rather than bringing it down by your side to throw it as you want your puppy to raise his head to look at your hand.

Allow your puppy to play with the toy for a couple of moments and then call him in, take the toy and repeat the game.

Build up the distance between you and your puppy by occasionally throwing the toy or the treat so that he never knows if it's still in your hand or 10 feet away on the ground.

Dogs love this game as they find it quite exciting... it's a great one to play in the house or the back garden as it's fun and full of focus and, once you've mastered it, you'll have an emergency stop that just could save your dog's life.

In time, and only once your dog is successfully stopping and waiting for his reward, instead of throwing it, walk to him, give him a stroke and have a play, so that you're building up his steadiness in the stop.

But wouldn't it be great if he could also

Although these exercises can be trained when your puppy is still a puppy, you've probably got enough to be getting on with training the basics, so cut yourself a bit of slack and introduce these when you can; think of them as added extras as opposed to must have's...

Come on the whistle

It's a great idea to introduce whistle commands at some point as the whistle carries further than the voice and tends to pierce through the concentration of even the most ardent of focussed sniffers!

As with the recall, training your puppy to come on the whistle can be done at home and in the garden as well as on your walks.

Any whistle will do providing it's not silent – we want to know our puppy has heard it as, if we're in any doubt, we'll blow it again and again until our puppy responds, in effect telling our puppy he can ignore the whistle until he decides to come. Nope, let's not go down that route, let's make sure we know our puppy can hear us and get a whistle we can hear too.

Call your puppy as usual and as he's running towards you double peep on the whistle and lure him in a little anti-clockwise circle to your left leg (or clockwise to your right leg) with a treat and into a sit. Give him his reward and tell him he's a good boy. You can then put his lead on while he's sitting beside you, walk him with you off lead or release him again for a play.

When you've got your puppy coming in to the heel position without too much help from you, you can use the whistle first as a means of recall rather than calling your puppy first; simply use your whistle!

My favourite all time whistle is the gundog whistle, which now comes in lots of different colours now rather than just boring black, so get the colour that you like with a matching lanyard to hang it from and keep them with your dog lead so that you always pick the two up together.

Whistle conditioning

You can speed up the whistle recall by conditioning your puppy to the sound of the whistle at mealtimes.

For the next week when feeding your puppy, stand beside the bowl to release him to eat; as he puts his nose in his bowl, very quietly peep-peep on the whistle and then leave him to it.

What you're doing is associating the sound of the whistle with his food, in the same way that Pavlov conditioned a dog to drool at the sound of the bell. Although his scientific methods were, by today's standards, rather cruel, any kind of pairing behaviours in this manner is still called Pavlovian (or Classical) Conditioning, whereas pretty much all other types of dog training fall under the banner of Operant Conditioning.

Stop on the whistle

When you've got your puppy stopping on command, you can add the whistle which makes stopping at distance so much more reliable.

The process is the same but, before you give your puppy his reward, pip or peep on the whistle. If you do this often enough your dog will associate the sound of the single peep with sitting or downing, depending on which position you opted for when training 'stop!'

Focus on me

There are loads of ways of teaching your puppy to focus on you, most of them involve holding bits of food up to your eyes, however, I shudder at the thought of potentially encouraging excitable young dogs to jump at my face, so I developed a different way of training it.

Pop your puppy into a sit facing you and let him know you have a treat in your hand; it can be a sweetie or a toy... whatever 'does it' for your puppy.

Take the hand holding the reward up to your breastbone, or hold your whistle, and as you do so, say a 'cue' word... it can be anything that you like – 'watch me', 'focus', 'eyes'; the main thing is that it feels natural and comfortable for you to say.

Have a little conversation (in a normal tone of voice) with your puppy, dropping in your cue word over and over again, for example, "good 'focus', nice 'focus', clever 'focus'" and then give him his reward before he looks away.

If you mistime it and he looks away before you get a chance to reward him it's not the end of the world, just set him up again with the lure and shorten the amount of time you're expecting focus from him.

In time you can move around while holding your hand to your breastbone and your puppy will stay focussed on you, regardless of whether he's sitting watching you, following you or walking beside you.

This is a great exercise to train and is fab to use on a walk if your puppy gets excited as you can sit him up and 'regroup' his energy and focus on you.

Fetch

Hopefully you'll have been doing this with your puppy anyway, this is just going to make it a little more formal... and a bit less stressful for you, as it will hopefully prevent your puppy from picking up a toy and taking off with it instead of fetching it back to you.

If your puppy has started running off with things, then let's set him up to succeed by attaching a long lead or a house line to his collar and have him sitting beside you.

Crouch down or kneel beside your puppy and hook a finger under his collar so that you can restrain him but without putting pressure on his neck; toss the toy and as it lands, or slightly before, remove your finger and say "fetch".

Encourage your puppy back to you by patting your legs and saying "come"; don't go over the top though as you could end up being too exciting and initiate a game of chase.

If your puppy doesn't want to bring the toy back, use the line to bring him to you, hook your finger under his collar, stroke him with the other hand, then take the toy and tell him what a good boy he is.

This early on in your training it doesn't really matter that you had to bring him back with the line – the important thing is that you're interacting with your puppy and your puppy is keen to play with you.

Don't overdo the game of fetch as not only can it lead to boredom, but you don't want to overly stress his young joints and ligaments.

If you find that your puppy doesn't want to play fetch, you can use a piece of equipment that I designed a few years ago called the Lez Graham Retrieving Roll, which is a roll-up strip of canvas with a treat pouch in it.

Used correctly it will quickly teach your puppy that the only way he can get to the treat is to bring it back to you and before you know it you can have a great game of fetch.

Because of the nature of the roll, it can be wrapped around toys and the like to encourage your dog to bring back other things too.

After half a dozen retrieves, not all at once I hasten to add, it's time to introduce the 'wait' command. Set up your puppy as before and this time pop him in a sit by your side.

As you go to throw the toy say "wait" and, after throwing the toy, count to three prior to sending your puppy; if he gets up before sending him for the toy then just pop him back into the sit position, say "wait", then send him.

The Working Cocker Spaniel.

Don't let the adorable cuteness of this breed fool you; he is a high
energy working dog who needs his brain exercised in order
to be able to settle down and relax.

The Four Pillars of Puppy Training

There are certain concepts that form the structure of any kind of learning as well as certain steps that we need to go through in order to master a new skill... and learning to train a dog is no different.

To make it easier to remember them, I've called them the four pillars of puppy training - these are the pillars that will support everything that you will ever do with your puppy.

Patience > Perseverance > Repetition > Habituation

Whether it's toilet training, training a new exercise or starting a new routine, keep in mind the four pillars of puppy training and you'll not go far wrong.

Patience

Although this one probably goes without saying, I'm going to say it anyway. Whenever we learn something new it takes a lot of slow methodical thinking; adding a physical element takes it to a whole new level... and that's just us learning how to train a puppy. When you add another sentient being into the mix it's a recipe for disaster. And so, my first pillar must be patience.

Patience with yourself and patience with your puppy...

Remember you're learning new stuff too, so cut yourself a bit of slack when you find it a bit challenging.

Perseverance

Don't give up. Take a break if you need to, but don't give up on your puppy... or yourself.

Your puppy wants to learn; be determined to teach him...

Your puppy's brain is a little sponge desperate to learn about the world he's living in; he's going to learn something today so make sure he's learning the right thing and make sure he's learning from you and not himself.

If you're getting frustrated, or your puppy's getting distracted, pop him in his crate with a toy, make a cup of tea and take five... then try again later.

Repetition

There are so many sayings about practice making perfect that are drummed into us while we're growing up that it's one of those things that we go 'yeah, yeah, I know'. However, for me, practice doesn't make perfect, only

Perfect practice makes practice perfect...

If what you're doing isn't working, repeating the same thing isn't going to make it right, it just means your puppy is going to be proficient at getting it wrong.

Imagine what you're trying to achieve (however small that is), imagine going through the steps to achieve it and then go for it.

Doing three, or even two, perfect sits is so much more beneficial than doing 10 silly, jumping all over the place sits; your puppy will be trained quicker and with a lot less frustration.

Habituation

I attended a Neuro Linguistic Programming training day earlier this year, and Brian Costello, the trainer, came out with a phrase that I thought summed up habituation perfectly, so I quickly made a note to include here. To habituate your puppy is to

Make the unfamiliar, familiar...

Regardless of what it is that is unfamiliar, part of raising our puppy is making him familiar with everything that is going to be part of his life; whether that's a laminate floor he needs to cross, walking alongside a busy road, passing a field of cows or seeing children running in the schoolyard.

A big part of making your puppy feel comfortable and confident in new environments, is to train your puppy in new environments using the four pillars of puppy training method.

When I brought my dogs to the UK from New Zealand in 2007, they went straight to Bart's breeder Jill. I knew that Bart would be fine as he was a strong confident dog that was going back home, however, I thought Angus, my Goldie, might need a bit of extra help.

I asked Jill that the second the transporting agent left the dogs with her to get Angus straight out on a lead and take him for walk, insisting that he walked nicely and for her to do a little bit of basic training with him; sit, stand and down.

Within minutes he'd settled on the lead and relaxed, trotting along with his beautiful tail swishing in time with his movement.

What we did for Angus was make the *unfamiliar, familiar.*

By taking him through a routine that he knew and felt confident doing, he could relax into the new environment quicker, knowing it wasn't 'going to kill him', which was pretty much Angus's first thought when going anywhere new.

K.I.S.S. your puppy daily

This acronym has been used for so many different things. If you know this saying, and are of a certain age, then you probably know it as "keep it simple stupid", which is how I knew it from my IT days, however, I changed it to **Keep It Short and Simple** for my puppy people and say to them to put a sign on their fridge to "K.I.S.S. puppy every day" as a way of reminding people to train.

Keeping it simple isn't just in relation to what we do with our puppies, it's about not overthinking the training too. We can get ourselves in a terrible muddle when we overthink it, making it much harder than it needs to be.

When I visit my puppy people I always end the training session doing this little routine to demonstrate how puppies follow the hand, or, to be more accurate, *wherever the nose leads, the body follows.*

Think about the collar height as being the starting point; above the collar is sit, level with the collar is stand and below the collar is down.

- To get your puppy to sit, slowly take the treat up and over his head
- To get your puppy to stand, lure him forward by moving the treat away from him at the height level with his collar
- To get your puppy to down, move the treat down and forward, taking your hand all the way to the ground to encourage your puppy's head as low as possible

Remember though, to train each exercise in isolation first so that your puppy doesn't think the stand always follows the sit and the down always follows the stand.

Dogs and Children, Children and Dogs

Children can have such a fabulous relationship with dogs and dogs in turn can teach children so many fantastic things; leadership, responsibility, love, friendship, kindness, sorrow... the list really does go on.

However, the relationship between our children and our dogs needs to be managed to make sure they both benefit, and yes, they do need to be supervised *at all times*... and yes, they should never be left alone together.

When I work with people who have dogs and young families, there's always resistance to this: "I trust my dog, he would never hurt my child", "they love each other so much my daughter climbs into his dog bed", "they play chase for hours", "my daughter loves to dress the dog up", and on it goes...

While this is all very lovely and straight out of a Disney movie, it really is a potential disaster waiting to happen.

I don't say this to frighten you or to add doom and gloom to the relationship. I say it to highlight how important it is to ensure our children and dogs have a respectful and safe child:dog relationship as opposed to the dangerous child:child one that is being played out as the 'norm' on social media.

Canines and Primates

Dogs are not fur-babies, they are social predators that have an innate set of rules. Their mind thinks differently to ours and they react so much quicker.

The way that they communicate is subtle and is often lost on us. Often, we only notice there is an issue when we hear the growl and see, and hopefully not feel, the teeth; whereas the dog would have gone through a range of communication signals *before* it got to that point; pause, frown, stare, freeze, glare, stiffen, change in weight distribution, puckering of the lips, growl....

Their skin is thicker than ours and they have fur protection; we have no skin on our body that is as protective as the skin on the dog's face or neck, the closest is the skin on the sole of our heel.

When a dog chastises another dog, or asserts dominance over another dog, they will quite often take a dog's muzzle in their mouths and hold it or give a squeeze; dogs do not shout at each other... when they bark it is a call to arms or 'back off' – they never 'tell each other off' by barking.

Children and Puppies

If you've got young children in the house, then it's really important to teach them to leave the puppy alone when he's sleeping, not to poke or prod at him, not to share their toys with the puppy and not to cuddle him. While this is an automatic human response it's not in the canine communication repertoire.

It does look lovely having a puppy snuggled against a baby, but only in our imagination; in reality, any movement from the baby can cause the puppy to jump on it, either because he got a fright or because he thinks it's a game or because he got hurt and is retaliating.

If you've got older children at home, teach them how to handle the puppy gently and safely, and teach them how to do some of the basic training.

Explain to them why it's important not to have the puppy on the furniture with them, but rather for them to sit on the floor with the puppy and for them take control of all the resources in a kind and gentle, but assertive manner.

Dogs and Children can have such a fabulous relationship... but only if there is respect from both sides and they are supervised at all times.

"When we start protecting our dogs from our children, maybe we will no longer need to protect our children from our dogs"
The Dog Safety Education Executive 2015

Puppies and Children

In the same way we need to teach our children respect around our puppy, so too do we need to say 'no' to our puppy.

Teach your puppy not to jump all over your children and your children's friends. Teach them that the children's toys are out of bounds for them and that it's really NOT acceptable to bite at pony tails, pigtails or dressing gown cords.

Instil good manners around feeding time by initially putting your puppy in his crate while the children are eating and later making him stay on his bed.

Keep your puppy on the floor and don't be tempted to have puppy on the settee with you, especially if you have a toddler: if your toddler comes over the settee to investigate, or is furniture surfing, then their face will be at the same height as your puppy and will be at risk of being inadvertently scratched or bitten as excitement rises.

When you see all of the safety tips written down you may have nodded and thought yup, all common sense... or you may have thought that it all looked a bit scary bringing children and puppies together... either way, you'd be right.

Having puppies and children in the home is a bit scary but mainly it's wonderful, and, as long as a little bit of common sense is applied with a lot of vigilance, you should be fine.

Just remember to keep these tips in the back of your mind, as they will help to keep your puppy safe from small, sticky, grasping, pulling hands and help to keep your child safe from small but incredibly sharp teeth and claws.

#putthecameradown

In Easter 2015, we ran a video-based campaign under The Dog Safety Education Executive (DogSEE) entitled #putthecameradown, to highlight the need for vigilance around dogs and children. The message behind it is that regardless of how 'cute' your dog and child are being, you need to be in the moment with them and not behind a camera lens videoing it.

If you have the chance, the videos are definitely worth a watch and can be found on the DogSEE website or Youtube.

Out and about with your puppy

Most of your early training will have taken place at home and no doubt you're itching to get out and about with your puppy, and who can blame you... it's wonderful going out with your bundle of fluff, but it's also really scary and full of what if's.

The main thing is to start small, do a bit of training in your back garden first after your puppy has toileted so he's a bit more focussed. Have the best training treats or his favourite toy to help as you're now competing against the exciting outdoors.

When you're ready, and there really is no rush, it's time to face 'the front door'. And for this we will go slowly, as our natural instinct is to charge out the door, down the path and onto the street where we expect our puppy to walk on the lead as beautifully as he did in the kitchen and the back garden.

Well, it isn't going to happen...

There's a very good chance that the second your puppy is standing outside the front door he's going to start jumping about or popping his head down and dragging you off for a sniff in every direction as his little nose, with its 220 million scent receptors are totally overwhelmed by the bombardment of new and intoxicating smells.

And this is where we stop. We do nothing, and we allow our puppy's nose to recalibrate to the new environment. If you have a big front door step, then take a seat and settle down for a few minutes or lean nonchalantly against the door and watch the world go by.

Sitting on your step or leaning against your door with your puppy in front of you, or beside you, is a good way to start exploring the world outside of your front door; he'll draw on your relaxed state and be able to take it all in while being still, rather than rushing through all the smells.

When you're ready, aim to do five or ten steps of walking on a loose lead, plus a couple of sits and then back indoors; that, coupled with standing still and chilling out for a few minutes really is enough for your initial training session outdoors and your puppy will be quite worn out by the new experience.

If you can, try to do this little routine three or four times a day, building up the distance that you go – don't aim to go around the block the first time out!

If you start this when your puppy is about twelve weeks old by the time he's sixteen weeks you'll feel as if you're 'walking the dog', however, walking or not – at this stage it's all about training and loose leads, not going out for a social gathering with friends; save that exciting treat for later... much later.

Age appropriate exercise

I'm often asked how much exercise to give a puppy and when to start training. The latter is easy; you started training from the second you brought your puppy home...

In relation to walking, the general rule of thumb recommended by the Kennel Club, is to add 5 minutes for every month of your puppy's life, so, if your puppy is three months old, the *maximum* he should be walked is 15 minutes; at 4 months it's 20 minutes and so on until you find a time and distance that suits your puppy's age and your lifestyle.

It'll probably feel like no time at all, and as soon as you get out of the gate you have to turn around and head back home again... and to start off with you'd be right.

Remember walking in the early days isn't about getting your puppy ready for a hike (or even going for one), it's about teaching your puppy how to behave on lead, introducing them to new sights, sounds, and smells, and making the *unfamiliar familiar.*

Once he's older, much older, and his ligaments and bones are stronger, then you can go power walking or jogging, but for now... work with adding five minutes a month.

Socialisation and Habituation

Socialisation and habituation are two sides of the same coin.

Heads is about ensuring your puppy is comfortable with his own species and animals of other species, including us; tails is about ensuring your puppy is comfortable in different environments.

Both heads and tails are all about making the unfamiliar, familiar.

Going for a coffee

From around twelve weeks I encourage puppy owners to get out and about with their puppies, a little sooner if possible. Now that's not going against veterinary advice of not letting puppies out before their second vaccination as I advise, rather strongly, not to put the puppy on the ground.

Find a nice café that you and your puppy can go to and while away a bit of time. I was spoiled for choice when I lived in Marlborough as we had a fabulous outdoor café and I used to sit with puppy Ziggy all bundled up in a towel on my lap and watch people, and the traffic go by, and, providing people asked first, he would get lots of strokes as well.

By the time Spud and Dante arrived, so had Café Nero, who are a dog friendly chain, and so my days of sitting outdoors ended and instead I sat inside by the window with the puppies on my lap.

When your puppy is a little older, is used to the lead and knows how to sit and down, park as close as you can to the café and do the same routine that you did when leaving your home for the first time; stand by your car until your puppy relaxes and then get your food treat and encourage your puppy to walk to heel to the café; there is no rush to get there, take your time and insist on a loose lead.

It's a good idea the first couple of times of walking to the café, not to allow people to stroke him as all that will do is build excitement which will make it harder for you to get your puppy to settle down when in the café and it means the next visit will be even more exciting.

When you get to the café, pop your puppy on a towel and either give him a stuffed kong and tell him to settle down / go on his bed or get him to sit or lie nicely beside you; when he's settled you can then use your leader's prerogative to decide who can and who can't stroke your 'sitting' puppy.

Teaching your puppy to do nothing

Sometimes we get so focussed about doing things with our puppy that we forget one of the most important things of all; teaching our puppy to do nothing.

You want your puppy to think that being with you is the best thing in the world; not just when you're being exciting and going on jaunts or doing some training... but when you're sitting reading a book, watching tv or surfing social media.

Likewise, when you're out and about; going for a quiet coffee, having Sunday lunch after a dog walk or simply sitting on a park bench watching the world go by.

At these times you want your puppy to just settle down or quietly amuse himself, being with you doing nothing. You want your puppy to think that hanging around with you is the best thing in the world; when you're on the move he wants to be too and when you're doing nothing he wants to do that as well.

Just in the way that you sat on the step with your puppy and stood at the car, then so too you're going to get into the habit of doing nothing out on your walks... and it is one of the hardest things in dog training to get into the habit of; when you're on a walk you want to be walking, when you're training you want to be training, not hanging around doing nothing.

Find a nice spot on your walk, stand still for a few seconds and watch the world go by... if your puppy starts to wander off, take a little step away from him and give him a gentle prod with a finger; when he comes back to you smile and continue admiring the view.

If a gentle prod isn't enough say his name in a fast, and almost but not quite sharp way, as you do so. He'll get the hang of it very quickly and the more you do it the easier it will be for your puppy to just chill out when you stop and do nothing.

'There's nowt as queer as folk'

... to quote the film The Full Monty. And it's absolutely right - people come in all shapes, sizes, colours and smells. They are bearded, bald, long haired, short haired, walk tall, crouch, limp, swing their arms, hide their hands, hum, whistle, frown and scowl.

Plus, we have the added appendages; long coats, short coats, padded coats, shiny coats, shorts, jeans, swishy trousers, skirts, hats, hoods, caps, scarfs, glasses, sunglasses, slippers, boots, high heels and roller skates.

And then we have the smells; shower gel, shampoo, soap, toothpaste, mouthwash, deodorant, shaving foam, aftershave, perfume, face cream, hairspray and fabric softener...

Just think about all the things that we use on a daily basis, changing how we look and smell and that is what our puppy needs to accept as part of us. A dog is a dog is a dog; but us?

Well, all we have to do is put a long coat on a we're a completely different shape altogether; a shape that our puppy has to add to his database as still being us.

And imagine how difficult it would be for them to see us in something like a bike helmet; morphing into some faceless alien creature with a massive head.

We owe it to our puppy to come into contact with as many of the above as possible (tick them off as you go); orchestrating it if needs be, so that when our puppy goes through his second fear period as a dog, he doesn't react negatively to a shuffling old lady walking past in a long coat, a floppy hat and a walking stick.

Meeting a friend's dog

Before you agree to a 'play date' for your puppy with your friend's dog ask yourself a couple of questions first. Is my friends dog well behaved? Is he a good role model for my puppy? Is he gentle when he meets people, or does he go a bit mad and jump around? Would I like my puppy to behave like him when he grows up?

Reading the list probably sounds a bit over the top to you, but bear in mind that you're introducing your puppy to a grown-up member of his own species; one that he will hopefully not only want to communicate with and emulate, but also one that won't scare or hurt him.

Meeting a new dog is always intimidating, especially for a young puppy, and so is best done in your own home if possible. Have your friend bring their well-behaved dog around to yours and leave your puppy in his crate.

When everything is nice and calm, and your friend's dog is in a down stay then let your puppy out of the crate; keep the dog in a down position if you can whilst your puppy investigates and then put the dog into a sit; before you know it, your puppy will be doing his own thing.

Please don't let them bound around and play as not only do you risk your puppy being hurt but you're teaching him that when a dog comes into your home 'all bets are off' and it's playtime; a gentle and calm introduction with a little bit of wandering around is the order of the day... there'll be plenty of other opportunities for them to play in the future.

Puppy Classes

Puppy classes come in all shapes and sizes and unfortunately, many of them can do more harm than good.

Puppy parties are generally nothing more than puppies being allowed to rough and tumble, teaching the small puppies to be scared of the big puppies and the big puppies to bully the little ones.

Socialisation classes can fall into the same categories of puppy parties but can be more educational, sometimes run by vet nurses in the vet's reception; however, unless the vet nurses are dog trainers or behaviourists they are not trained to train you or your puppy.

Find a good local trainer, a trainer that is recommended or known for sensible training that uses positive rewards as well as common sense consequences, and one that doesn't parade the puppies round on head collars and harnesses, or allow the puppies to hoon around at the end (or beginning) of the session.

In an ideal world you're looking for a smallish class that lets you sit with your puppy on your lap or by your feet on a little mat, educates you on what a puppy is, helps you through the little problems that puppies bring and teaches you how to train your puppy to walk on a loose lead, sit, stand, down and come.

After that, tricks are great, providing they're age appropriate and not going to damage your puppy by pushing him too far too soon. However, if tricks are all the puppy class is going to give you then you're better off finding someone else.

Harsh? Perhaps... but I've seen so many gorgeous dogs ruined by attending puppy parties and badly run training classes.

In all honesty, the owners would have been better off working through a socialisation plan on their own and making themselves the centre of their dog's universe, rather than spending time and money walking round and round with a piece of food in front of their puppy's noses.

Expecting the Unexpected

From the second you take your puppy outside, whether that's in your arms during the early days, or trotting along beside you at four months old, mentally you need to be prepared for life's little challenges.

And I don't mean challenges from your puppy, I mean dog walking in the real world.

At some point you're going to come across the bouncy off lead Labrador that wants to play, needs to play and positively insists on playing, or you're going to come across the dog-less person who lives in hope of meeting dogs on their daily walk so that they get to cuddle, stroke and be jumped up on...

Both things that can send you and your puppy into orbit; the first can do lasting damage to your puppy's personality and the second can do some serious damage to the training of your puppy and your relationship going forward.

Dogs

I can guarantee at some point you're going to have to deal with dogs when you're out and about; it could be a well-mannered dog with a responsible owner (fingers crossed for lots of those), an unruly dog at the end of a flex-lead or an off lead out of control pain in the proverbial.

When you see a dog try to keep walking, at least initially. Take charge of the situation and position yourself so that you are between your puppy and the other dog, and try to ensure there's a bit of a gap between you so that should the dog lean towards your puppy, he's not going to clatter into your legs.

Make yourself more interesting to your puppy as you're walking, using your voice or, to help you out in the early days, a little piece of food. Your puppy may show interest in the other dog, which is natural; tell him he's a good boy, keep walking and encourage him to do the same.

When your puppy can happily walk past a dog on the field or in the street then it's up to you when you decide if he can have a sniff but up until then I wouldn't encourage it.

You want to be the most exciting, most important thing on your dog walk and if you let your dog say 'hello' to every dog you meet on your travels, then that will become the highlight of the walk and your dog will, instead of 'hanging out' with you, start looking for other dogs... depending on his personality, he could start pulling you towards them or lunging at them wanting to play.

When you come across an unruly dog, at the end of a lead, it's really important that you take control. If you feel concerned that the dog is going to reach your puppy, ask the owner to give you a bit of space and keep walking.

You need to demonstrate to your puppy that you are strong enough to protect him (if he's feeling a bit worried by the situation) and are in control (if he starts messing about) otherwise you run the risk of your puppy getting worried by over-exuberant dogs or behaving in the same manner.

If, or rather when, you come across an off lead out of control pain in the proverbial, protect your puppy. Lifting your puppy up could make matters worse as the loose dog could start jumping up at you to get at your pup, which will at best fluster you and unnerve your puppy, so if you can, leave your puppy on the ground.

Position yourself between the dog and your puppy and call of the dog's owner. If the dog is being friendly and sniffing calmly then quietly stroke your puppy and keep him calm until the owner arrives and then quietly set off about your way; you want to make this as much of a non-event as possible, so that your puppy isn't unnerved or over excited by the encounter.

If, however, the dog is unruly and jumping all over your puppy, and unfortunately this does happen, then you have a few choices.

- You can try telling the other dog to 'go away' and point away from you - this works sometimes but watch the dog's reaction, you don't want to trigger a negative response in the dog or scare your puppy.
- You can try holding your lead quite close to your puppy and swing your lead in an upright circle in front of you, thereby forming a barrier between you, your puppy and the nuisance dog. I would practice the lead swinging at home without your puppy at the end of it if you live in an area that has lots of unruly dogs.
- You can try my favourite deterrent and throw a full poo bag towards the loose dog which will make him back off – just remember to pick the poo bag up afterwards.

Most of your dog walks will be a pleasure but, as the saying goes, 'forewarned is forearmed', and if you can stay calm your puppy will too.

People

I can't say enough times that your puppy is *your* puppy and *you* decide who he says hello to and who he doesn't, whether that's a human or an animal. Please don't feel obliged to let all and sundry stroke, pet and generally ruin your pup.

Most people love puppies; they bring out the child in us, and so tend to go over the top when interacting with them, unwittingly causing no end of training and behaviour issues for the owner.

'Way back when' it was considered rude to stroke a dog without first asking permission from the owner; now it seems to be rude for the owner to say that they don't want strangers to stroke their dogs or puppies... ridiculous really when you think about it.

You are going to have to let your puppy say hello to people as part of his education and integration into our society, and, depending upon the breed and personality of your puppy, you're going to have to let him say hello to a lot of people or you're going to have to restrict the amount of people he meets; however, that doesn't mean he meets all and sundry and it doesn't mean he meets everyone on his terms.

Make a point of not letting him say hello to everyone you pass, say a cheery hello as you walk past and say something like "training," so you don't feel as if you're being rude, if that works for you. You can now get high visibility vests made for your dog with 'In Training' or similar, printed on it to help deter friendly hands if it all gets too much.

Every third or fourth person that you meet that shows interest in your puppy ask if they would like to stroke him, or if someone is well mannered enough to ask, then say yes on the condition that they help you train him; which means getting your puppy to sit for attention and stay sitting the whole time the person is stroking him.

Please don't let the stranger give your puppy food... You'll end up with a dog that once let off lead, is mobbing everyone he comes across thinking they've got a sweetie for him – it is one of the hardest habits to break, so please don't encourage it now.

Everything else

If you see joggers or cyclists on your travels, and I really hope that you do, take a step to the side, position yourself so you are between your puppy and the jogger or cyclist, and put your puppy in a 'sit'. Keep him sitting as the joggers or cyclists approach and go past... and really go past, not just until they're level with your puppy.

Dogs, like every other predator on the planet, are only interested in 'the chase' once something has gone past them and is moving in a direction away from them.

When something is running at them or towards them, they don't know if they are the 'prey', however, when that animal has passed, and bear in mind that we are animals too, then the predatory instinct comes to the fore and the instinct to chase kicks in.

Do everyone a favour, including your puppy, and teach a solid sit-stay around moving objects and animals, and if you do come across horses or cows in a paddock, don't take your puppy over to say hello, as you could end up teaching him that when he sees them off lead he's supposed to run over and say hello... and then mayhem *will* ensue.

The School Run

When my son was at primary school I had a puppy, and when Bart was old enough, I used to pop him in the car a couple of times a week and take him on the school run with us as part of his education and then call into the park on the way home.

Having him with me at the school gates worked out well for everyone; for me and Bart it meant he had to learn how to relax while children ran past shrieking and how to sit nicely while children came over to say hello; for other parents and their children it meant that they had to learn to ask if they were allowed to stroke a dog and not just rush over and hug it... woe betide the child that launched itself at my puppy!

I'll never forget an incident when Bart was 5 months old though; we'd dropped Callum off at school and then drove to the park on the way home which was where the mums used to meet after the school run. They would stand in the middle of the green throwing a ball and all the dogs would run after it, or they would just stand and have a gossip while the dogs hooned round and round them.

It was very rare that I used to join them, preferring to walk Bart around the outside of the park on the pavement, teaching him to walk on lead and ignore other dogs. It was round about this time that I'd been a spectator on my first shoot and had fallen in love with 'the gundog', or rather the 'picking up dog' and was determined that Bart was going to follow in his mum's footsteps.

This day however, and I've no idea why, I decided to go and join the mums in the centre of the circle of dogs. I wandered over with Bart on lead and was standing chatting to a mum, admiring her son's new bicycle, when out of nowhere, this huge 10-month-old lurcher made a beeline for Bart.

I can only presume because the dog had been hooning around the adrenaline was up and rather than stopping when he reached us, rammed Bart straight into the bicycle, puncturing Bart's right tricep on the pedal as he did so. Here started two months of rehab as Bart needed stitches and then got a seroma (a pocket of fluid that can happen post-surgery) which needed to be drained.

I thought I would share this snippet as a way of highlighting how easy it is for things to go wrong when we stop being vigilant with our young dogs; I literally took my eye 'off the ball' for a few minutes to talk to a mum and Bart got damaged... and although the lurcher was only being over-exuberant and didn't have a nasty bone in his body, he managed to really hurt my young dog.

Luckily it was only physical damage and not psychological as had Bart not have been a mentally strong, confident puppy, it could have really affected how he was around other dogs or he may have associated the pain with the bicycle and become frightened of them or attacked them.

Keeping your dog safe

When I was growing up it was the norm to see dogs tied up outside of newsagents or lying outside of greengrocers waiting for the owner to come out.

I used to do it with my first dog when I went to the shops to get the newspaper for my dad. Kym would wait outside for me and then carry the paper home in her mouth, sometimes walking to heel and other times I used to have her walk the low narrow walls that went around people's gardens and jump from gate post to gate post without dropping the newspaper.

But it was a different world then; dogs in the UK were allowed to roam the streets up until 1990 when the Environmental Protection Act came into force - people were a lot more relaxed about dog ownership, letting the dogs out in the morning for a wander, or to chill out in open, unsecured gardens. Kym used to walk me to the corner when I went to school, hang out in the garden until lunchtime when she used to come and meet me at the corner of my street to carry my bag home, repeating the routine in the afternoon.

We couldn't do that now and I, for one, wouldn't want to do that now... I want to keep my dogs safe at all costs.

Dogs outside of shops

Tying a dog up outside of a shop isn't against the law, although it could be argued that by tying him up you're taking away his freedom from running away from danger (and therefore in breach of the 2006 Animal Welfare Act) but it is incredibly irresponsible... for so many reasons.

The amount of times I've seen children go over and hug a dog that they don't know that is tied up outside of a shop. I've challenged parents of children for allowing it to happen and I've challenged children.

It only takes the dog to turn quickly and for a child's face to be in the way and that child could be scarred for life... and the dog destroyed.

I've also challenged people untying their dogs, asking if the dog belongs to them. Dog theft is on the rise with certain breeds being stolen to order; stolen so they can be bred at puppy farms for the 'designer' dogs or stolen as bait for training fighting dogs.

Never leave your puppy tied up outside of a shop.

Walking by roads

If you walk your dog by the side of the road he should be on lead. It doesn't matter how well trained your dog is he should be on lead; and I mean a short (not tight) lead, not an extended flex lead.

If you walk your dog off lead or on an extended flex lead, then you must accept that you are taking a massive risk and that at some point your dog could end up under a car.

Dogs are predators and it only takes a moment's lapse of concentration from you with a badly timed cat running across the road and your dog could be dead.

I've had to brake a number of times for dogs on extended flex leads wandering off the kerb to investigate an interesting smell on the road - and the owners have been helpless to do anything.

Please, please, please... take heed of the warnings and keep your puppy, and then your dog, safe...

A Recall is a Recall is a Recall

One of the greatest pleasures of dog ownership is watching your dog running around being a dog, playing fetch or just watching them explore somewhere new.

Before we can do this though, we need to make sure that our dogs come when called and, being realistic about it, our puppy will be an adolescent dog by the time we let them off lead.

However, that doesn't mean we can't do some serious recall training with our puppy by starting a bit of longline training with him, although at this age, unless he's a larger breed dog, you might be better off using a light two or three metre house line.

Because the house lines are so light you are able to walk your puppy on them all the time. A little game I like to play with puppies while training the recall on a house line is...

As you're walking along with your puppy on a loose lead, take a couple of steps backwards quickly and say "'puppy' come" and keep walking backwards with your puppy walking towards you.

You can either stop and pop your puppy in a sit, then put him to heel and keep walking, or, turn away from your puppy and continue walking to heel for a few paces before turning and walking in the direction you were originally going.

Because your puppy won't know when the game is going to start, he'll be more focussed on you during your walk, and as well as having a bit of fun on your walk, you're training a recall.

Longline training

As well as being fun, your recall should also be unconditional; your recall should not only make your young dog think "yay!", he should also be thinking "how fast", as opposed to, "in a minute..."

So, if your puppy isn't coming back quickly from the garden when at home then do some longline training with him before you consider letting him off lead in the real world.

A longline is a longer, thicker, heavier version of the house line that you may have used when your puppy was younger. It can be a bought line from a pet shop which generally come in lengths of 10m and 15m, a lunge line that you use with horses or a homemade one of rope with a spring clip attached.

I made my first longline from bale twine when I was 13, it must have been at least 300 yards long as it stretched quite easily from one side of the hayfield to the other. I just tied it on to Kym's collar and then removed it when I put her regular lead back on.

The main thing to remember with longlines, shop bought or homemade, is not to tie yourself up in it and never let it lie on the ground behind your legs, plus, if it's thin or your youngster is big and fast, to wear gloves.

Walk on a loose lead to a suitable field or area where you want to give your puppy some freedom. Attach the longline (then remove the lead) and walk about 20 paces or so with your puppy by your side on a loose lead. Give your release command and let your puppy go out, up to the length of the line.

The longline must never have tension; as your puppy gets towards the end of the line, give it a quick flick or a gentle tug.

You can then say, "Puppy come" and bring your puppy in to sit in front of you, give him a stroke and a food reward before putting him to heel and heeling for a few paces before releasing him to play again or put his lead back on.

Or you can peep your recall whistle and have your puppy come to your heel, reward and walk a few paces before releasing him to play again or put his lead back on.

Thinking ahead to when you have your dog off lead, sometimes you'll not want him to come all the way back for a stroke or his lead on, sometimes you'll just want your dog to catch you up or change the direction he's heading in.

To train it you would simply keep walking in the direction that your heading and give the longline a little flick (or a gentle tug) and say something like 'puppy this way'; he will run to catch up as soon as he realises he's been left behind. Verbally praise at distance and continue walking with a loose line.

Another really valuable command to teach as part of your longline training is 'too far', for when your puppy is too far in front of you - give the line a little flick (or a gentle tug) as you say "too far" and verbally praise as he comes back within a decent range.

Depending on how often you walk your puppy, and how often you do the training, will determine how many weeks it will take to condition a good recall, however, if we base this on walking your puppy twice a day incorporating some longline training on each walk you can adjust it accordingly, then...

Do the above on every walk for 2 weeks. On the 3rd week drop the line and allow your puppy to drag it behind him... not only will it slow him down a bit but if he doesn't respond immediately you can stand on the longline for immediate control. If you feel confident with the recall at week 4, then remove the line.

If you don't feel confident, then replace it with the shorter houseline; as your confidence increases you can start shortening the line so that he just has a short lead attached, that way he can feel the touch of the 'line' and still feel attached to you, otherwise continue letting your puppy drag the line behind him until you're confident, as regardless of what you believe, you will be right...

If you think your puppy will come when called (and you've trained him to do so of course) then he will, and if you think he won't come when called, he'll pick up on the weak energy and will do his own thing.

Never do longline training in the forest, or where there are a lot of bushes, as it would be really easy for your puppy to get caught up and hurt his neck and back.

Don't be shy with your praise - the more exuberant the better. Don't be afraid to use a jackpot (many treats one after the other each accompanied with a "good boy") when training a recall and always use high value treats.

When you give your puppy a food reward, give the treat with one hand and stroke him with the other. Remember he's not allowed to go play again without permission.

If you work your longline training around the psychological development stages of your puppy, then you'd be starting the training around 16-20 weeks, just in time for the Flight Instinct Period (see Living with an Adolescent).

The Border Collie.

The 'classic' sheepdog, the border collie can still be seen working
sheep in many parts of its native Britain. Highly intelligent with high drive
and energy, this dog is not for the sedate family and does extremely well at
intensive sports like agility and competitive obedience.

Puppy Problems

Every puppy is unique.

Even within the same litter the difference in personalities is vast, and when you add to that the different environments and lifestyles that the puppies are homed to, the list of problems that people face can be seem truly daunting.

However, some of the challenges we face with our puppies are universal and it's the universal ones that I've tried to cover. Jumping up, mouthing and chewing are the three things that drive most puppy owners to distraction, as not only do they hurt, but they can put children off dogs for life if they're on the receiving end of sharp little teeth and claws.

Please do keep in mind though, that for most puppy problems **vigilance is key,** and **prevention is better than cure.**

If you're watching or interacting with your puppy then he can't be sitting chewing the new table; if your puppy's in his crate, then he can't be sitting chewing the table... if you can't keep an eye on your puppy then for everyone's sake, keep him out of harm's (and mischief's) reach and pop him in his crate.

In the same way that children will pick things up and then put them in their mouths, so too will puppies pick things up and chew them.

At some point everyone gets frustrated with their puppy and wants to rant and rave; it's human nature to do so... but before you do, try to look first at what you could have done to prevent the problem and what you can do to *prevent the problem in the future*.

Jumping up

The only way to successfully combat a young puppy jumping up is to train a really good sit, and be really consistent about not stroking your puppy until he is doing so.

If he does jump up, ever so quietly put his front paws back on the ground and pop him in a sit position. If he is insistent, then slide the palm of your hand down his chest and as you do so hook your thumb into his collar so that he can't ping up towards you. He may struggle a little and that's okay, just calmly stroke him and tell him he's a good boy as you gently restrain him.

Avoid bending down over your puppy and having your face low and towards him as it may encourage him to jump up as he tries to greet you by licking at your mouth; instead, try to go down on your haunches (rather than kneeling) keeping your face away from your puppy's and be prepared to prevent him from licking you as this is the contact he wants.

If your puppy is successful in repeating the behaviours he enjoys, in this case jumping up and licking your face, he will be even more determined to keep doing it.

Things like scarves and dangling earrings are best avoided at this time, as well as fancy cuffs and flouncy hemlines, as these are irresistible to a puppy who just see's these items as PLAYTIME!

Mouthing

Mouthing is, unfortunately, something we all have to go through with our new arrival as it was part of his communication with his litter.

He needs to learn how much pressure to put through his bottom jaw when using his mouth; whether that is on a toy to make it squeak or on a chewy to bring relief to his teething. He also needs to learn how much pressure on us is acceptable behaviour or unacceptable behaviour, in the same way that he learned it in his litter.

It's not something that can be avoided or something to get angry or exasperated about, although you will... it's just something that every single puppy owner has to go through.

Once your puppy is home *and settled*, the first time you feel his little teeth on you, shriek and I mean SHRIEK, as loud and as high pitched as you can (in general though, rather than leaning towards him and shrieking in his face) and get up and walk away from your puppy with a look of absolute disgust on your face.

In the same way his litter mates would, you have just said to your puppy that he plays too rough and you're not interested in being with him.

He will look totally bewildered and may run in the opposite direction or he might just sit with a comical look on his face, however, regardless of his reaction, your only reaction should be one of disgust - it is really important that you don't stay near him and I can't stress enough how important it is not to laugh.

Give it a minute or so and then make yourself available for a cuddle again, however, if puppy does it again then make sure you repeat the procedure and give him a longer time out.

If it continues then put him in his crate for a time out in there, and no, he won't associate the crate with being a bad place; that only happens if you shout and scream at him as you put him in it.

If you have children, or a very determined puppy, then you can put some Gannicks bitter apple spray on the cuffs of jerseys, socks and hem lines but apply it away from the puppy, so he doesn't see it happening, and make sure you flood his senses with it initially as detailed below.

Chewing things

Puppies are notorious for chewing I'm afraid; it's what they do. In the way that babies explore their environment by picking things up and putting them in their mouths, so too do puppies lick and chew them.

When children go through teething they rub their gums back and forwards on their fists, your arm and pretty much anything else they can get in their mouth to give relief.... well puppies are the same.

When dogs chew, their brains are flooded with happy hormones which are very soothing for them, so as well as finding out new and interesting things and relieving teething pain, chewing calms them down and helps them to settle.

I can remember when Bart was a puppy and we went out for dinner leaving him with our friend's son who was babysitting for us. I went through all the puppy stuff with him before we went out, you know the crate, toileting, feeding, all that is apart from, yup, you've guessed it, chewing.

We returned from a lovely night out to find that our furniture had been well and truly crimped by sharp little puppy teeth. Luckily, he hadn't taken any chunks out, just left perfect little teeth marks all the way round an ottoman and a table... which are still there 15 years later.

Your puppy has no concept of 'posh' wood, to him wood is wood is wood, and that lovely polished table leg will probably be just as nice to chew as the manky old stick in the garden, although likely not as tasty, so do yourself a massive favour and don't let him chew sticks when in the garden, or anywhere else for that matter.

Not only will chewing sticks give him a taste for wood, but he could also end up with splinters in his mouth, get the stick jammed on the roof of his mouth, or perforate organs if he swallows it - **sticks and dogs, contrary to popular belief, do not belong together.**

The Deterrent - Gannicks Bitter Apple spray

This is my all-time favourite deterrent for chewing and mouthing. Citronella spray is also pretty good, but it means we have to walk around smelling of citronella, whereas we can't smell the bitter apple.

I also tend to keep the citronella spray for later, for when a young dog takes it into his head that jumping up on the settee with you may just be fun, which is normally around the four or five months old mark.

This is the bit that I hate, but it works so well and makes the bitter apple such a powerful ally in your fight against mouthing and chewing. Take some kitchen roll, saturate it with bitter apple spray and then give it a shake to take the excess off.

Very quietly, and without speaking or smiling or anything remotely reassuring, gently hold your puppy and put the kitchen roll over his nose – he will try to pull back from it or wriggle as to him it smells vile.

Keep it there for a couple of seconds then remove it and use it to wipe down table legs or wall corners or anything else he's been nibbling at before popping it the bin and giving your hands a good wash.

Then pick up one of your puppy's toys and have a little play, or a cuddle. The key to doing this is to act as if nothing is wrong; if you 'baby' your puppy now you'll be affirming that there's something to be worried about and you'll be praising his hesitancy.

When your puppy is not around spray the bottom of all your furniture, especially table and chair legs, corners of skirting boards and anything that you think may be appealing for a puppy, including your hands if you have a 'piranha puppy'. If you're spraying soft fabrics remember to do a colour-run check first.

Now forget that you ever conditioned your puppy to the bitter apple and your puppy will too... that is until he tries to chew one of the treated areas... and then yuck!

The dreaded dishwasher

There are some photos of dogs and puppies that are guaranteed to make me cringe - the ones of them licking the dirty plates in the dishwasher.

Some people think it's really funny to let their puppies lick the dishwasher dishes and some people don't. I've seen people struggle to keep their dogs out of the dishwasher and I've seen dogs guard the open dishwasher and growl at their owners.

If you do have a puppy that simply cannot resist the lure of the smells coming from your dirty dishwasher, then there is an easy, no-fuss fix.

Have a full glass of water sitting on the bench directly above the dishwasher. Leave the door down when you have dirty dishes in there, staying over by the bench as you do.

Watch your puppy from the corner of your eyes and when he comes over to the door upend the glass of water into the door; do it silently, do it fast with a wrist flicking action as if you're pouring it down the sink, and then put the glass back on the bench.

What we're aiming to happen is that the water hits the open door fast, bounces off the door and splashes your puppy; he won't be expecting it and will jump back; because you're silent and have totally ignored the proceedings, it will be between the dishwasher and your puppy.

If you do this whenever your puppy goes near the dishwasher (set it up a couple of times throughout the day) then the consequence for trying to lick the dirty plates is an unpleasantly wet one, instead of a yummy licky one.

Begging and 'greeding'

Dogs will only beg or greed for food if they are fed from your plate, dinner or bench... simply eating in front of your puppy won't cause it.

Your puppy might look at you hopefully initially, especially if your food smells amazing, and let's face it, pretty much everything will smell amazing to that little nose, but he should then abandon hope fairly quickly and move on... if he's ignored that is.

If you make a fuss of him or give him a bit of whatever you're eating, he'll come back for more, and more, and more. And if you make him wait, and then give in and give him some, he'll hang around for longer thinking that's what's expected of him.

Dogs won't waste energy on things that don't benefit them in some way; if sitting in front of you while you're eating doesn't get them a reward of some kind (a stroke, a smile, a bit of food) then they will give up. If, however, you chat away to them and give them a bit of your sandwich, they're going to be there, waiting and drooling for a piece of the 'spoils'.

Stealing

As hard as it is to get your head around; dogs don't steal... ever. They may take something from the table, out of the bin, from another dog or even from your plate... but they're not stealing.; **stealing is a human concept.**

A dog is an opportunist with the classic 'see it want it take it' mentality, but, and it's a big BUT... they will only do it if they're allowed to do it. And by that, I mean that the reward for taking it outweighs the consequences.

This is why, from a very early age, while your puppy is very malleable we teach NO. It's much easier and far gentler, to teach a young puppy no as described earlier than to indulge them and then have to come down firmly when they hit adolescence.

The key as always, is prevention by being vigilant and not giving your puppy the opportunity to take things that you don't want to him to have.

Train the 'leave it!' command and train 'fetch' because then if you see your puppy heading towards something he's not allowed, you can move swiftly towards him with your fiercest face while growling 'leave it' and using the hand signal. As soon as your puppy leaves it or turns away from it you can reward him with a big smile and a happy recall.

If you're a little late and he's managed to pick it up, don't get drawn into a game of chase (which is that all-time favourite of canine games) call him to you as you would when playing fetch; invite him into your game rather than being a player in his. Remove the item and check there's nothing else lying around that might take his fancy.

Hoovers and Hairdryers

Both hoovers and hairdryers can cause so many issues with dogs. I don't know if it's the noise, the vibration or the movement, but I've worked with dogs that have run away and hidden from them, and I've worked with dogs that have attacked them; both instances are fear driven.

The most important thing when dealing with these two household items is to not make a fuss and, if you have children, don't allow them to make a game of it with the puppy.

Start with your puppy in his crate and don't hoover too close or use your hairdryer right beside it. Ignore your puppy and get a little bit closer every few days.

If your pup is reacting fearfully, then leave the hoover or the hairdryer in the same room as his crate and play with your puppy beside it; make a game of throwing toys and treats in the vicinity, and praising your puppy for going and getting them. Sit beside the hoover or hairdryer and give your puppy a treat from beside them.

Build up with the hoover so that you're walking your puppy beside the hoover while the hoover is switched off and eventually when it's switched on.

If your puppy shows any kind of aggression toward the hoover or the hairdryer then quite sternly say 'NO!', and work on desensitising them as if you ignore the behaviour it will only continue, and if anything, will get worse.

What every puppy owner should know

The saying, "we don't know what we don't know" rings true for pretty much everything in life and it doesn't matter how much studying or observation that we do, there are always things we don't know... and don't know that we don't know them!

So, even if you think you know about the things that follow, skim the chapter anyway, just in case...

How dogs learn

The dog's brain works in a very similar way to ours, in that it has neurons, synapses and neural pathways, however, it doesn't have the same 'components' that ours has.

Human beings have two areas in their brains that allow verbal speech. Broca's area which is associated with the production of language and the spoken word, and Wernicke's area which is associated with the processing of the words that we hear. Both areas are named after the scientists that discovered these functional areas of the left hemisphere.

Without getting overly technical, these two areas are connected by a large bundle of nerve fibres resulting in the human production and understanding of speech; if either of these areas are damaged then the spoken word is affected, that's presuming of course that the larynx, or voice box, is working effectively.

As we evolved to stand upright, our windpipe developed a 90° angle and it is this bend in the throat that allows the voice box to be lengthened to make different pitches of sounds; the dog's windpipe however, only has a slight bend to it.

We also have a rounder, larger tongue than a dog, whose is reasonably short and flat making it impossible to curve around into the necessary position for complex vowel sounds.

It is because the dog is lacking these two communication areas that they can't be reasoned with; they simply don't understand the words that we are saying to them. Everything that we teach our dogs is an action conditioned to a sound; they cannot make the word connections that we can... 'sat' and 'sitting' have no relationship to 'sit' unless we condition them to mean the same thing.

One of my favourite all time quotes, and one that is never far from my mind, is by the philosopher Bertrand Russell who observed that, "no matter how eloquently a dog may bark, he cannot tell you that his parents were poor but honest"; only words can do that....

The Times Tables

Can you remember back to your school days and learning how to multiply using the times tables? 1x2 is 2; 2x2 is 4; 3x2 is 6... over and over, pretty much every day?

If you had a good teacher, they made it a bit of a game and if you didn't, then it was a bit of a drag all round, but either way it worked; *you learned your times tables*.

That is one of the ways that we, and our dogs, learn. It's called rote learning or learning through repetition and it's a way of drip feeding information into long-term memory.

What happens when we learn through rote, is that slowly and surely, we develop neural pathways in our brain that become more established through use, until using them becomes an automatic response.

And, if we're doing something physical, not only do we get a neural pathway for the activity, but we also get something called procedural, or muscle memory, where the proprioception system stores the 'feeling' and sensory information of what we're doing.

Remember when you learned to ride a bike... you had to think about everything you were doing; keeping your balance, watching where you were going, keeping the handle-bars straight and pedalling - all at the same time!

As you learned this new skill you would have been really wobbly, but hopefully had a parent or a relative holding onto the back of the saddle to stop you from toppling over once the stabilisers came off to help with your confidence before letting you go and watching you ride your bike.

As the saddle was released you would have been a bit tentative, as your body was learning how to balance in the new precarious position; the muscles would have been constantly talking to your brain and your brain constantly talking to your muscles.

Neurons would have been passing chemical messages (neurotransmitters) across the synaptic gap to other neurons up and down the neural pathway, in the way that runners in a relay race pass the baton.

And in the same way that the relay runners get faster and more proficient at passing the baton, so too do the neurons get more adept at passing signals up and down the pathway making it more efficient, more travelled and the 'go to' path for a particular action... in this instance; riding your bike.

The same but different

But what if you decide to ride your friends bike and your friend has a racing style road bike whereas yours is a BMX mountain bike?

Well the established pathway will still be used, but it will add more information to it; a change in the angle of the knee and the thrust of the thigh due to the pedals being in a different position... and maybe the arms are held differently as the handlebars are in a different position.

The basic skill (riding a bike) is the same, but it's different, and you've had to make adaptations. *You're not learning a new skill, you're enhancing an old one.*

This is why, once we have trained an exercise, we then need to train it again in different environments; *same exercise different location*. Initially you'll have to train it from scratch, however, once you've trained the exercise in a couple of places your puppy will have adapted the established pathway to include other stimuli and training in new places will become easier.

Unconscious conditioning

In the same way that we consciously drip feed behaviours into our dog's brain, so too do we *unconsciously* drip feed behaviours into our dog's brain.

As creatures of habit we tend to use the same words when doing the same things, and for the most part we tend to think out loud; as a predator, dogs instinctively watch for nuances and patterns. When we combine our behaviour with our dog's behaviour we end up living with an animal that knows what we're going to do as we think about doing it.

For the most part your dog will ignore you as he will learn very quickly that you're not talking to him and your voice will fade into the background (which is why walking around talking at your dog is not a good idea), until you say a word that normally precedes something exciting.

I had, at some point, got into the habit of saying "right then" before I got up and did something; it didn't take long before my dogs picked up on it and would be on their feet waiting before I'd even finished the 'then'.

Another thing that I unconsciously conditioned my dogs to, was ripping off a sheet of kitchen roll. I know... huh? Well, I went through a stage when Dante was a puppy of wiping their faces over with a bit of damp kitchen roll and giving them a treat for sitting nicely as I did so. Dante wasn't really a touchy-feely puppy, so I did everything I could to teach him to tolerate and enjoy touch.

As a result, every time I ripped off a sheet of kitchen roll I had three dogs run into the kitchen and sit nicely waiting for their faces to be cleaned – and their treat to be forthcoming.

The big bang

Another way of moving the information into long term memory is by the big bang approach; information that is wrapped up in high emotion.

Getting a big fright by something or someone will generally go straight into long term memory as an automatic survival response. Let's just say you've learned how to ride your bike and are out and about on it. If you were to pull out in front of a car and that driver blared his horn at you it's unlikely you'd do it again because the memory has been slammed straight into long term memory due to the emotional impact.

For our puppy it could be that we dropped something very loudly on a hard floor beside them and then over-fussed them; the noise (fright) plus our reaction (high emotion) would put the incident straight into long term memory and we would have to then work to change the reaction, desensitising the response.

Unintentional conditioning

I can remember years ago unintentionally conditioning my goldie Angus to be afraid of wasps.

I was working in the office and a massive, noisy wasp came in through the window heading straight for me. Well I did all the right things of course; I was on my feet waving my arms at it trying to shoo it back out of the window shouting "out, out" as I did so.

Did it work? Oh yes.... Angus was standing shaking in the hallway. I felt dreadful as I hadn't considered that Angus, who was fast asleep in his bed at the time, would have been affected.

It was only later that I realised how affected he was, when every time a bluebottle, wasp or bee came into the room, he would run out.

The Four Pillars of Puppy Training

If you can keep in mind the Four Pillars of Puppy Training, then you won't go far wrong training your puppy.

Patience and **Perseverance** are really for you. **Repetition** is putting the new action into long term memory and **Habituation** is adapting the new action to new environments or simply taking it a bit further.

Good Puppy, Lovely Puppy, Naughty Puppy

Something that can really put the kibosh on our training is good puppy syndrome... or cute puppy syndrome... or gorgeous puppy syndrome.

When our children are behaving well or are doing all that we ask them to do, we tend to cut them a bit of slack knowing that they understand why we have, and also, that we can reason with them if their behaviour deteriorates because of it.

Unfortunately, that's not an option with our puppy.

The only thing that cutting our puppy a bit of slack will do is cause our puppy's behaviour to go downhill. Repeating commands (once taught and 'understood') and not insisting on our puppy carrying out those instructions, will only teach our puppy to ignore our wishes and become unruly.

So regardless of how good or lovely your puppy is, keep training the behaviour that you want, and keep insisting that you get it.

Optimum Health

Puppies will do whatever they are capable of doing, and whatever they are able to get away with. That doesn't mean however, that they do what is good for them, or that they know best.

Puppies will keep going until they literally keel over from exhaustion, then get up and keep going again. All that does for them is to make them fractious and potentially damage their bodies as they're not equipped for sensory overload.

If you can remember that your puppy is very much a little baby in terms of physical needs you'll be halfway there; like babies needing morning sleeps and afternoon naps, so too does your puppy need time in his crate to rest and assimilate all that he's been learning.

We prevent our children from climbing over things and going upstairs for fear of them falling, but foolishly encourage puppies to do so. Climbing, jumping up, bouncing around on hindlegs and going up and down stairs are all dangerous for your puppy as not only could he fall but he will be causing unnecessary strain on his joints and ligaments.

At the point of writing this (Winter 2017) the research project Pupscan, was investigating the impact of repetitive exercise, jumping up, and knocks and bumps on the puppy's hips and elbows, and whether they are more of a contributing factor in joint disorder in adulthood than was previously thought. Until we know for sure that elbow and hip dysplasia are purely down to genetics, then we need to do everything we can to prevent damage to our puppies.

To me however, it makes perfect sense that a bump, a bang, or twisting a joint will potentially cause issues later; the ligaments (connective tissue that attaches bone to bone, think cruciate ligament) aren't as robust or tight as in adults, hence the saying loose-limbed when describing young animals.

Although we want our puppies to be puppies, and not wrap them up in cotton wool, we need to do all that we can to prevent damage to the growth plates, which are positioned at the end of the bones and made of cartilage. As your puppy develops, they get denser and calcify, however, before then, your puppy is at risk of damaging them, either through a knock which could cause a fracture, or compression damage which can be caused by the two soft bone ends hitting each other hard, which could happen if your puppy jumps down from a height.

The growth plates are very much open in our puppies, closing, depending upon breed, between 8 months and two years; the larger the breed the later the plates close, the longer the dog is susceptible to damage.

So research when the growth plates close for your breed and restrict the repetitive games until then; be strict about not allowing your puppy to run up and down stairs and be mindful of what activities your dog takes part in – the last thing you want is to rupture a ligament or damage a growth plate.

The former will need surgery and months of rehabilitation, and the latter will potentially alter future growth, resulting in a lopsided dog.

In one end, out the other

According to the 2017 figures released by the Pet Food Manufacturers' Association (PFMA) Pet Data Report 2017, there are around 8.5 million dogs in the UK equating to 23% of all households owning a dog.

Through the course of the year they ate 835,000 tonnes of food at a value of £1.3bn.

Whichever way you look at it, dog food is big business; there are an awful lot of manufacturers looking to get your hard-earned cash and they will go to incredible lengths to get it.

Years ago, a photographer I used, was approached by a dog food manufacturer to see if they could use Ziggy on the cover of their dog food bags and then as part of their marketing campaign. My photographer said he would ask but it was highly unlikely I would say yes as I didn't feed their food. He was right, I said no...

The majority of dog food manufacturers are only interested in the bottom line and most of them are owned by large multi-nationals that make many other things; for example, coffee, chocolate, ice-cream, washing up liquid and washing powder. Dog food is just another product in their portfolio.

They aren't necessarily aware if the dogs that they use in their advertising campaigns are fed the food that they're advertising or not – they're just looking for really healthy, athletic looking dogs to make the food look more appealing and increase their sales... because, as I've already said, "dog food is big business".

But where does it leave us dog owners, trying to do the best for our dogs? Well, we find out as much as we can about our dog's nutritional needs (which will change over time) and learn how to read dog food labels. Our dogs condition and behaviour will tell us if we've got it right.

Hopefully when bringing your puppy home, your breeder will have given you some information about what he's being fed and hopefully it will be good sound information. I can remember getting Angus' food chart when I brought him home and put it straight in the bin; Weetabix with milk for breakfast, marmite on toast for lunch and raw mince for dinner. I think not.

Your puppy should be on four meals a day until he's three to four months old when, depending upon breed, you'd drop it down to three meals by slowly increasing breakfast and dinner slightly and replacing supper with a little biscuit (I tend to give my puppies a Winalot shape for bed).

At six months old, again depending upon breed, you can reduce the meals down to two by splitting the lunchtime meal between breakfast and dinner and then it's really up to you if you want to reduce meals to one a day at ten months or continue feeding twice a day. I feed my dogs twice a day as it works well for me and my family.

That was the easy part, the difficult part is figuring out what to feed; raw, wet or kibble?

For me as an avid raw feeder it's a no-brainer; I feed an excellent quality complete and balanced raw food. I haven't got the skill or the patience to balance my dog food myself so instead I buy one that has been done for me, defrost it and feed it with a little bit of mixer that has been designed to complement a raw diet.

I understand that for many, raw feeding isn't feasible and so, for me, the next best thing is a good quality complete and balanced wet food mixed with a good quality grain-free mixer. Lastly, I would feed a good quality complete and balanced kibble.

The most important thing though, is to feed the best **complete and balanced** diet that you can afford; which means that the food has all the vitamins and minerals in it that your dog needs for good health, and, those components are balanced for the life stage / breed of your dog.

Diet and nutrition are complex and emotive so if you need advice try to go to someone impartial or get a couple of different opinions and do a bit of research yourself.

Your puppy, and then your dog, however, will tell you when he's on the right diet as his coat, breath and stools, as well as energy levels, will all indicate if you're feeding what he needs.

Your dog's coat should be shiny, and his skin should be conditioned and not dry; many dogs throw dandruff when in stressful situations and is commonly seen on black dogs when at the vets... this is a biproduct of stress and not necessarily related to diet.

Your dog shouldn't smell, not even when wet; you might get a fresh clean/damp smell but not the nose-wrinkling gut turning wet-dog smell.

His breath should be inoffensive as should his poo, which should be firm and hold together when you pick it up; it shouldn't be smelly and sloppy.

Your dog should have good energy, even high energy; but not manic... so, if your dog has smelly farts, bad breath, sloppy poo's and is running around like an idiot, it's time to look at his diet.

Grooming

Depending upon your puppy's coat, you should, in the early days, be fine using a baby's hairbrush and I would always recommend starting with something similar as you want grooming to be such a lovely, relaxing thing for your puppy and not a massive stressor for you both and wading in with a stiff brush or metal comb will do just that.

Grooming is a time of bonding and checking for lumps, bumps and injuries so find a time when you can relax on the floor with your puppy and settle down... but wait until after their mad half hour and are a bit sleepy.

Start brushing their back or shoulders as that's the least tickly area and with your other hand keep your puppy steady with slow gentle strokes while restraining him with a thumb in the collar if needs be.

Settling down and grooming (or fiddling and faffing) on a daily basis is best but not always realistic, so try to do it three or four times a week and make a note on your calendar or in your diary to help you remember.

Time really does fly by and if you don't make an effort now to teach your puppy to relax and accept the attention, you could come unstuck further down the line as your youngster tells you in no uncertain terms that he doesn't want to be groomed.

Creepy Crawlies

There are certain parasites that love dogs and it's our job to keep our puppy parasite free. Your breeder would have wormed and de-flea'd your puppy while in the litter and hopefully would have given you instructions on what was required next - if not, talk to your vet.

The main things we need to watch for are worms, fleas and ticks; the latter are mainly a summer nuisance, but, depending on where you live, can be around most of the year as they only hibernate when the ground temperature drops.

When I lived in the south of England we would get ticks all year round, however now I live in Scotland, I only really see them in the summer.

Please don't overdo it with the flea and worm treatments once your puppy matures, as pumping your dog full of chemicals can't be a good thing, and moderate them whenever you can... I tend only to treat for ticks, for example, when I've found a couple on my dogs over a short period of time, rather than applying tick treatment month in, month out all year round.

Vaccinations

Depending upon your breeder, you may be bringing home your 7-8-week-old puppy having already had his first vaccination – let's hope not as his immune system will be very immature at this early stage in his development and many vets, my own included, like to wait until they're 9 weeks old before they start their immunisation programme.

However, as the UK law now states that dog breeders must ensure that puppies are microchipped and recorded on the microchipping register by the time the puppies are 8 weeks-old, and before they are sold, breeders might get the puppy vaccinated at the same time.

Vaccinating your dog, like vaccinating your child, is a very personal and emotive subject, and I have friends who vaccinate their dogs and friends who don't; I also have friends that vaccinate until their dog reaches a certain age and then stop, however, the majority of them all agree that regardless of whether you're going to vaccinate ongoing or not, the puppy vaccines are a must.

I know you may be reading this and thinking you should always vaccinate, or you may be reading this and thinking you should never vaccinate and go down the homeopathic or herbal remedy route, however, as a behaviourist all I'm going to say is do your homework, weigh up the pro's and the con's, talk to your breeder and talk to your vet... and then make an informed decision.

To Neuter or not to Neuter; that is the question

The term neutering applies to both sexes; for the boys it's castration, where the testes are removed and for girls it's spaying, where the womb and ovaries are removed.

From pretty much the time you bring your puppy home, you're going to start receiving all sorts of uninformed advice about neutering; about how it should be done before the hormones kick in to prevent him wandering and being aggressive, or if you have girl, that she should be spayed prior to her first season... none of this is true.

Your puppy's hormones are there for a reason and that is to turn them into adult dogs; they make the males male and the females female, and they tell the growth plates to close and for the dog to stop growing.

So please, wait until your dog is an adult and have an informed talk with your vet, your breeder and your trainer, and then make an educated decision.

Be diligent in your training, set your boundaries, practice leadership and apply common sense and I can't imagine you'll encounter many problems; if you do then go back and read this book and be honest with yourself – are you falling into the Good Puppy, Lovely Puppy, Naughty Puppy syndrome, as that's normally at the root of the problem.

If you're still not happy, get a canine behaviour practitioner out for a consult (see useful contacts), then, and only then, consider neutering for behaviour issues.

As a behaviourist I work with so many dogs that have behaviour problems that have been made worse by spaying and castrating at a young age, and which could have been resolved by behaviour modification training... behaviour modification and a very large dose of common sense that is.

If you have a vet that is encouraging you to castrate or spay at six months, you might want to do some research, have a chat to them and then, if needs be, consider changing vets.

Dogs and the Law

Dogs are the only animal on the planet that have their own specific set of laws pertaining to their behaviour. Whether they are in relation to noise, livestock, fouling or biting, the laws are there to protect us, and others, from dogs being a nuisance or a danger in society.

I had planned on including the main laws that apply to dogs here, however, they have been in a state of flux over the last few years with updates to the Dangerous Dog Act and the Dog Welfare Act to name but two. It was also announced this week that the Scottish and English governments are going to join Wales in banning the electric dog training collar (Wales banned it's use in 2010).

To find out about dogs and the law, the first place to look is the government website followed by your local council website to find the byelaws relevant for your area; the Kennel Club also have an up to date section on their website, although they do tend to pepper the information with emotive comments.

The French Bulldog.

With his larger than life personality and compact size, the 'Frenchie' is
quickly becoming one of the UK's favourite breeds and has been close on
the heels of the gundog breeds in popularity for the last couple of years.

Living with an Adolescent

You made it! You made it to the other side of Puppyhood, well done! Now gird your loins and strap yourself in for *Adolescence*.

Adolescence is often referred to as the Juvenile Period which starts at around weeks 16-18 but depending on breed can be as late as week 20, so, keep in your mind that life with your puppy will change between four and five months.

Just like with children going through adolescence and friends becoming more important to them, so too will other dogs hold a greater interest for your adolescent dog and he'll want to go off and play with them.

That doesn't mean you let him, in fact the opposite is very important during these next few months, as not only is this known as the Play Instinct Period, when play is high on the agenda, but it's also categorised as the Flight Instinct Period – **the time when your dog is most likely to take off.**

Whaaaaat?

Yup...after *all* of the hard work you've gone through with your puppy training, the hormones have kicked in and your dog will want to take off; it just doesn't seem fair does it?

Teething... again?

The other major thing that is going to happen in your dog's life during this period is that his big teeth come through, and I hate to say it but if you think puppy teething was bad then take a deep breath because this is when your dog needs to really work his jaw.

Most of his front teeth will be cut by this time but starting at four and half to five months, his canines will come through followed by his molars and premolars. If you haven't dealt with 'mouthing' by now, then you need to get professional help as he will be biting hard to try and relieve the pain and frustration of the gum irritation.

He'll be teething until he's around ten months or so, which is when the teeth are set in the jaw, and the jaw and his mouth start to settle down; until that time give him access to hard chew toys or palmate antler chews, which as you may guess from the name are quite simply antlers. The palmate ones are flatter, tend to be softer and are less likely to damage young teeth as the dog gnaws at them; save the big hard ones for when your dog's big teeth are well and truly established... or

better yet, give your dog a brisket bone which are the soft rib bones –
but remember bones are always fed raw and never cooked.

The Teenager

Adolescence is well and truly at home with hormones flying around,
when your dog gets a second whammy of becoming a teenager and
goes through the classic 'Kevin' phase.

If you haven't seen the Harry Enfield character Kevin then I suggest you
search the internet and watch the clip where Kevin becomes a teenager
as it will give you a really good idea of how your darling puppy is going
to transform over the next few months.

Although I've anthropomorphised it a bit, it's really not far off the truth;
most of the dogs that are handed into rescue centres are around 10
months old – presumably the owners simply couldn't take the teenage
months any longer.

It's all happening now, and as well as behavioural changes and growth
spurts due to hormones, at some point between six and fourteen
months your dog is going to go through his second fear impact period.
Also known as the 'fear of new situations period', it doesn't really have

a 'set' time frame for arrival... quite simply one day your dog is fine, the next day... not so much.

I can clearly remember two of my dogs going through it and although I can't recall situations with the rest I'm sure they must have gone through a milder version.

Angus was around the fourteen-month mark when we moved to a new house. We were living in New Zealand at the time and we moved from a rural'ish area to town; it had a busy'ish road not far away, what I would class as a typical UK 'B' road.

Many days were spent just hanging around on the corner of our street with Angus while he went through all manner of reactions to traffic... although he'd seen and been walked around traffic before, it wasn't quite in such volume.

After a few weeks everything was cool for Angus and traffic no longer posed a problem for him. Then one day he almost wrenched my arm out of its socket as he leapt sideways and away from a concrete post; it didn't move, it had always been there, but today, for some reason unknown to me, it had become the scariest thing on earth.

Ziggy went through a similar thing when he was around ten months. Always an inquisitive puppy he grew up into a confident and enthusiastic adolescent, always keen for doing something new and even the boring mundane stuff like emptying the washing machine was exciting. That was until one day when I took a shirt out and shook it... all of a sudden it was a monster that was going to eat him – he shot out of the kitchen and stood shaking in the sitting room.

"Here we go again" is what went through my head.

So, what did I do? For both dogs it was a case of firstly not making a fuss, and secondly, desensitising them to the situations.

With Angus it was a case of walking in ever decreasing circles around the concrete post, a little every day until I was leaning against it; when he relaxed and stopped looking at it out the corner of his eye I gave him a treat, well many treats actually but only when he was relaxed. I also threw treats near the post for Angus to go and get.

With Ziggy it was a case of calling him to me when I was crouched by the washing machine and giving him a treat; taking an item of clothing out of the machine, giving it a wiggle (rather than a shake) and rewarding him for not reacting. I slowly built it up over a couple of weeks so that I could shake out clothes again without him being worried.

In the same way you didn't reassure your little puppy you shouldn't reassure your grown-up dog and make a fuss; just carry on with the same 'nothing to see here' attitude and you'll get through it.

Don't force the issue either as your dog is genuinely scared of whatever it is that's unnerved him, so slowly and without fuss, desensitise him as you did when he was a puppy.

In the way that the start date is woolly, so too is the end date and there will be times when you feel as if you're walking on shifting sand. The best advice I can give at this time, is be patient and go with the flow; lead by example and show that there is nothing at all to worry about.

I've found that the second fear period tends to coincide with a growth spurt or a hormonal surge, so with dogs watch out for it round about the time that they start to cock their legs to urinate and with bitches around the time of their first season.

Stepping up to the mark

As you might guess, this is the time when your young dog is going to potentially test boundaries and get selective hearing... and yes, you might just end up pulling your hair out.

But try not to despair; the stuff you have taught your dog is still in there, it's just buried under hormones, and well... even more hormones.

You might notice during these next few months that the well-trained, delightful puppy that you were so proud of, has morphed into an untrained, unruly, boisterous dog, who, while lovely is also pushing every one of your buttons.

You might find during this time that your dog is...

More interested in everyone and everything. Make yourself important. Fun and games are definitely on the menu, but only if coupled with boundaries and leadership. You bring the toys out and you put them away. Revisit the Leave it! command if he tries snatching toys off you; if he won't bring them back, pop him on a longline, a houseline, or play with him only when he is on lead so that you are in control.

Backchatting. If your dog is barking at you when you tell him off or tell him to do something put him in his crate... and take a breath. Then spend the next few days with your dog on lead with you. Normally when a youngster barks back like that it's because you're interrupting something they are enjoying or getting them to do something they don't want to do (I know, you're thinking teenagers and rolling your eyes aren't you).

A couple of days of realising that you're in charge won't hurt him, although it's a bit of a drag for you. The key to this little exercise is to not fuss him, just go about your normal tasks with your dog in tow.

Ignoring you. You tell him to go on his bed and he just looks at you; you tell him to come and he just looks at you... and on it goes. If you're at this stage, then it's a case of keeping him on a longline while out and about and revisiting your training. If you haven't already done so condition your dog to come on the whistle.

If it's a case of him not responding around the home, then as you tell him to do something, start moving towards him at the same time... so if he's lying in the middle of the floor and you tell him to go on his bed (for whatever reason) be expansive; point to the bed, look at the bed and walk towards your dog, in effect herding him onto the bed if you need to. Make it absolutely clear what you want him to do.

Stopping halfway through doing something. He may have forgotten what he was supposed to be doing. It sounds daft but there it is. If your dog is surrounded by amazing smells he might have simply gotten distracted rather than being naughty.

His brain is being bombarded by all sorts of things at the minute so for this one, cut him a little bit of slack and repeat the command... if he ignores you then you can go for it as above.

Full of beans. Yup, your dog will have boundless energy at the minute; you'll feel as if you've just got back from a walk and your dog is hassling you to go out again. Don't. Don't fall into the trap of overwalking your dog now. He is still in his growing phase and you don't want to overdo it... instead be inventive with games and up the ante with your training.

If he will do a down stay for 10 seconds, set yourself a goal of 5 minutes; never quite got the stand? Now is the time to train it. Play fetch, teach him to catch... Brain training is so much more tiring than walking or running around - all that will give you is a fit dog with good stamina that will need even more walking.

Clingy. It can happen – your confident, outgoing puppy can become clingy. If this is the case, teach him to stay on his bed as it will help him to relax in his own skin and stop you feeling as if you're tripping over him all of the time. Try not to over fuss him as it may be the start of his second fear period and you want him to come through it confident and not jumping at his own shadow.

Be consistent

During the puppy training days, we tend to be really consistent with our commands, however, when our dogs have a command we start to be sloppy; 'down' becomes 'lie down', sit becomes 'sit down' and 'come' becomes 'come here'.

We all do it because we know other people 'get' what we're saying... but dogs don't. They don't have 'that part of the brain' and so we need to be really consistent with our commands *all of the time*.

Changing them around can cause confusion, and if your young dog is confused, it's because you're not being clear, and if you're not being clear, how can your dog do as you ask?

Be insistent

If you've asked your dog to do something, then make sure that he does it. That doesn't mean getting all growly or aggressive – if you've told him to go on his bed and he doesn't, then lead him by the collar and put him on there; then ask yourself if you've trained the exercise properly, or if you need to do a bit more training, or even go back a step or two in your training. **Never give a command that you cannot insist is carried out.**

Be persistent

Yes, I know, you told him to sit stay, he got up, you put him back and he's got up again... put him back again; never give up, to do so will only make your dog persist in doing his own thing.

Remember this is a predator that you're dealing with and they have the hunter's mentality of never giving up; if they gave up hunting because they didn't catch anything they would die...

Being consistent, being insistent and being persistent are all absolutely key when training a dog, never more so than when you're training your *teenager.*

Shall we dance?

However, the teenage months can be such a wonderful time to really get to bond with your dog, and develop a fabulous relationship with him as you up your game with his training and take it to the next level.

As our dogs become more and more responsive and pass through the gawky gangly stage, we can really feel as if we have a companion that will watch our backs and 'walking the dog' can have a real primal feel to it, allowing us to get back to nature and in touch with our inner nomad.

But walking a dog can bring with it stress too, especially if we have a puller, and so, to the final piece of training...

Start off with your dog on whichever side he normally walks on; as he gets slightly ahead do a quick about turn, turning away from him so that he stays on the same side. As you do so gently but quickly give the lead a little double flick and keep walking.

When your dog has caught up and is walking nicely beside you, say 'heel', smile at him, and keep walking for a few paces before repeating the exercise, so that you continue heading in the direction you want to go in.

For me, loose lead walking is a bit like doing a dance, with you leading and your dog following.

I went to dancing classes years ago and as my hubby was delayed I had the honour of working with Alison, the instructor. Something she said stayed with me and I've applied the principles to dog training ever since... she said, "Allow yourself to be led".

And that's what we're doing with that little double flick on the lead as we turn; we are saying to our dog 'allow yourself to be led'. We then put ourselves into the leadership position by putting our shoulders back and striding out; dictating the pace and the direction of the dance... or in this case the dog walk.

Regardless of what we do, when we do it with someone or something else, one person takes the lead, and the other follows; so, step up to the mark, and lead the dance...

Expect your dog to be well behaved and enforce it positively and in a way your dog understands, and you will end up not only with a dog that is looking to you for guidance and leadership... but you will end up with a dog that is a joy to own.

About the Author

Lez has an M.A. in Professional Practice (Canine Behaviour & Psychology), is a Fellow of the Canine and Feline Behaviour Association and is a master trainer with the Guild of Dog Trainers, as well as a Touch for Health Instructor and an NLP practitioner.

Lez's focus is on training the next generation of dog trainers and behaviourists, and empowering others to be the best that they can be, regardless of whether that is through helping people at home with their wayward dogs, teaching them Touch for Health, or coaching them through self-development protocols...

Lez lives in South Lanarkshire with her husband and her two gorgeous gundogs.

Useful contacts

The Kennel Club
www.thekennelclub.org.uk

British Veterinary Association
www.bva.co.uk

The Pupscan Project
www.pupscanproject.org

The Dog Safety Education Executive
www.dogsee.org

Dog Training and Behaviour
The Canine & Feline Behaviour Association of Great Britain
www.cfba.co.uk

The Guild of Dog Trainers
www.godt.org.uk

Lez's websites
www.lezgraham.com
www.braidwoodbooks.com
www.thepetgundog.co.uk